AF413699

The Ledger and The Land

Slavery, Wealth, and the Black Cherokee Economy Before and After Removal

The Ledger and The Land

Slavery, Wealth, and the Black Cherokee Economy Before and After Removal

Part of

the Black Cherokee series

Ty "GWY" Wilson

A Cherokee historian from the Cherokee Nation of Oklahoma

[BLK-FTHR Media/PE Church]

CHEROKEE NATION, USA

Copyright Page

BLK-FTHR Media/PE Church

© 2026 Ty "GWY" Wilson

This work is nonfiction. It is based on historical research, public records, and community memory. Names of public figures and parties to public legal proceedings appear in a historical context. All errors are unintentional.

ISBN: 979-8-9889198-5-8

Printed in the United States of America

First Edition Hardback

Dedication

For the descendants of mixed Cherokee and Black ancestry who are Black Cherokees

For the descendants of Cherokee Freedmen, who stand today as Black Cherokees.

For the ancestors whose labor built value that was never counted in their own names.

For every family that kept receipts in a Bible, a cigar box, or a memory until the world was ready to see them.

For every Cherokee Elder that has worked to preserve our culture and history.

For every historian that has helped to preserve the Native American narrative.

I say "**Wado**" (Thak you)!

I dedicate this book to you.

Epigraph

We were in the fields, in the ledgers, in the treaties, and in the fire.

The only place we were missing was in the telling.

Table of Contents

Contents

Author's Note on Method and Terms

This book is written from inside the story.

My work grows from three main sources:

- the archival record, including Cherokee, federal, state, and local documents

- published scholarships by Cherokee, Black, and other historians

- a Black Cherokee research matrix and datasets that I have built over the years, combining census data, treaties, Dawes records, maps, newspapers, oral history, and economic case studies

I treat this material like a ledger. I am less interested in whether the past was polite than in what it did on the ground.

How I Use Key Terms

Language has changed over time. The law changed. The people did not.

To keep that clear, I use three related terms in precise ways.

Cherokee Freedmen

In the nineteenth century, this term referred to Black men, women, and children who had been enslaved by Cherokee citizens, or who lived as free Blacks in the Nation, and who were emancipated under Cherokee law and the Treaty of 1866.

The treaty promised that these Cherokee Freedmen and their descendants "shall have all the rights of native Cherokees." When I write about the period from emancipation through allotment, I use "Cherokee Freedmen" to match the legal language of that era.

Descendants of Cherokee Freedmen

This phrase describes the children, grandchildren, and later generations of those original Cherokee Freedmen. It appears most often in twentieth and early twenty-first century legal and political contexts, because that is how courts, statutes, and tribal documents refer to them.

Black Cherokees

Citizens of the Cherokee Nation who also have Black ancestry. In history, there were Black Cherokees in the Nation who were recognized as being by blood. Their descendants are still considered Black Cherokees today.

Also, in the present tense, descendants of Cherokee Freedmen are Black Cherokees.

They are citizens of the Cherokee Nation under the 1866 treaty and the 2021 Cherokee constitution, just as U S Freedmen descendants are Black Americans. Cherokee Freedmen descendants are Black Cherokees

Throughout this book, when I am speaking about the present, or about a continuous people across time, I use "Black Cherokees" as the living name.

When I am speaking inside a specific legal or historical moment, I use the term that applies in that moment, and I name the connection:

- in the nineteenth century: Cherokee Freedmen

- across multiple generations: descendants of Cherokee Freedmen

- today: Black Cherokees

How I Use "Black," "Indian," and "Native"

Race and identity in this story are complex. Many people in the historical record had African, Cherokee, and other Native or European ancestry. The record often flattens them into one box.

I follow a few simple rules.

- When law or record uses a term that carries force, I quote it, then unpack it.

- I do not erase Black ancestry where it mattered for how a person was treated.

- I do not erase Cherokee or Native ancestry where it mattered for citizenship, kinship, or land.

When I use "Black" on its own, it refers to people read and treated as Black in their time, including Black Cherokees and other Black residents of Indian Territory and Oklahoma.

When I use "Native," "Cherokee," or the names of other Native nations, I am referring to political and cultural identity, not blood percentages on a card.

Method: How I Read the Record

This project rests on a mix of:

- quantitative reading: acres, valuations, census counts, crop yields, insurance claims, and court awards

- qualitative reading: narratives, affidavits, oral histories, and the silences between them

I treat gaps in the archive as information. When a record lists every slave by first name and price, but never acknowledges their children or their work in building a house, that omission is part of the story.

I do not use Wikipedia, the Cherokee Nation public website, or the 2026 Task Force report as primary interpretive sources in the body chapters. Those appear in the conclusion and the appendices, where they belong as contemporary reflections and receipts.

The core narrative is grounded in:

- Oklahoma Black Cherokees by Karen "Coody" Cooper and Ty Wilson

- *The Cherokee Freedmen: From Emancipation to American Citizenship* by Daniel F. Littlefield Jr.

- *Ties That Bind: The Story of an Afro-Cherokee Family in Slavery and Freedom* and *The House on Diamond Hill* by Tiya Miles

- foundational works by Theda Perdue, Fay A. Yarbrough, Claudio Saunt, and other scholars listed in the bibliography

- archival collections at the Cherokee National Research Center, the Sequoyah Research Center, the Western History Collections at the University of Oklahoma, and related repositories

Whenever I give a number, a date, or a legal claim, it sits on at least one of three supports:

- a primary document

- a recognized scholarly work

- a calculation based on those two, with the assumptions stated in the text or notes

Style and Limits

I write in my own voice. I do not pretend to be neutral about slavery, dispossession, or massacres.

What I do promise is:

- no invented evidence

- no romanticizing of any side

- no use of clever language where clear language will do

The record we have is imperfect and uneven. Black people appear in it most often as property, occasionally as witnesses, sometimes as plaintiffs, and rarely as authors.

This book is one attempt to answer that imbalance. It turns the scattered mentions into a ledger, and it reads that ledger from the standpoint of Black Cherokees.

If you see your ancestors in these pages, I hope the terms I use feel accurate and respectful. If you disagree, then the conversation continues, which is how living history should work.

INTRODUCTION

Why a Ledger Tells the Truth

Stand in almost any story about Black Cherokees and Cherokee Freedmen and someone is counting.

A slave trader counting bodies in a pen in Georgia. A Cherokee planter counting acres cleared and bales pressed. A federal agent counting heads for rations on a removal road. A Dawes clerk counting names for the final roll. A Greenwood shopkeeper counting cash at the end of a long Saturday.

The numbers slide around. Who is counted, and how, keeps changing. The pattern underneath does not.

This book begins with a simple conviction.

If you follow the ledgers, you will find the truth that the official stories try to avoid.

From Morality Play to Balance Sheet

Most people learn this history as a morality play.

Noble Indians driven off their land.
Cruel slaveholders and suffering slaves.
A tragic removal called the Trail of Tears.
A jump cut to Tulsa and a "riot" in 1921.

In that version, the economic details sit in the background.

Slavery is treated as a moral stain, not as an economic system that built measurable wealth. Removal is treated as pure dispossession, not as the transfer of real assets from one set of owners to another. The Treaty of 1866 is treated as a political bargain, not as a document that turns people from property into citizens with claims on land and money. Greenwood is remembered as a tragedy, not as the deliberate destruction of a dense Black business district.

This book does not ignore the moral weight. It refuses to stop there.

I am interested in what the work was worth.

How many acres were cleared.
How much corn and cotton were grown.
How much land changed hands.
How much money in lease payments, oil royalties, and insurance settlements moved in which directions.

Once you ask those questions, you leave the safety of the morality play and enter the harder terrain of the balance sheet.

The Four Questions

The chapters that follow all circle four questions.

Who created the value.
Who recorded the value.
Who captured the value.
Who was locked out or written out.

You can apply those questions to any scene.

In a Cherokee household in the early nineteenth century, an enslaved Black woman planted and harvested the fields that made her owner rich. She created the value. The account books recorded it under his name. He captured it. She was written out, even when she appears on the same page as a number, such as "woman aged thirty."

In Indian Territory in the 1870s, a Native Freedman family fences eighty acres along a creek and brings it under cultivation. They created the value and, for a time, they captured more of it. They show up on census rolls and in tribal records as landowners, which is a different kind of entry.

In Tulsa in 1921, Black residents build a neighborhood full of homes and businesses. White mobs burn it in less than twenty-four hours. Survivors file insurance claims. The companies deny them. The city moves on. The value created is obvious. The value destroyed is measurable. The gap between the two is the story.

The ledger lens is not a trick. It is a refusal to let the plot drift away from the people who did the work.

Why Black Cherokees Are at the Center

There is a reason this book focuses on Black Cherokees and Cherokee Freedmen instead of trying to cover all slavery and all Native history in one volume.

Black Cherokees and Cherokee Freedmen sit at a crossroads where African and Native histories meet, where slavery and sovereignty meet, where federal, state, and tribal law overlap and collide.

They were enslaved under a Native government that itself was under pressure from the United States. They were freed into a Nation that depended on their labor and often tried to limit their claims. They used treaty rights and land policy to build real wealth in a way that most Black Southerners were never allowed to do. They then watched many of those gains stripped by allotment, state policy, and violence.

Because of that position, Black Cherokees give us a clear view of how race, law, and economics interact.

If you want to know what happens when you give formerly enslaved people real access to land under a communal system, you can study Cherokee Freedmen farms.

If you want to know what happens when you give them citizenship in a tribal nation and then try to back away from that promise, you can read the Native Freedmen lawsuits.

If you want to know what happens when you block them from capturing the full value of what they build, you can stand in Greenwood in 1921.

The point is not that Black Cherokees suffered more or less than anyone else. The point is that their history gives us a sharp instrument for seeing how power and property have moved in this part of the world.

How the Book Is Built

The book moves in roughly chronological order, but it is not a straight line.

Part I looks at slavery and wealth in the eastern Cherokee Nation and treats removal as a form of asset destruction.

Part II looks at the rebuilding of the Cherokee Nation in Indian Territory and the way emancipation and the Treaty of 1866 created a new and fragile status for Black people as citizens.

Part III follows communal revenues and allotment and shows how identity categories such as "by blood" and "Cherokee Freedman" became filters for wealth.

Part IV drops down into Cherokee Freedmen labor and enterprise and uses case studies, especially the life of Zachariah "Zack" Foreman Sr., to show what Black wealth looked like when it was allowed to grow.

Part V traces the connections between Black Cherokee economies and urban Black districts such as Greenwood, then walks through the destruction and rebuilding of Black Wall Street as an economic event, not only as a racial massacre.

Part VI pulls the threads together. It follows the money across the whole arc and presents a Black Cherokee economic atlas that maps farms, towns, institutions, and routes, then sets out in plain terms the difference between value created and value captured.

The conclusion and epilogue bring that analysis into the present, where treaties still matter, descendants of Cherokee Freedmen are still arguing their status, and Greenwood is still a live question in law, politics, and memory.

Who This Is For

I wrote this book for three overlapping circles of readers.

For Black Cherokees and Cherokee Freedmen descendants who know pieces of this story from family and community and who want to see their people treated as central actors, not as footnotes.

For Cherokee citizens and Native readers who want a clear account of how slavery, emancipation, allotment, and Black wealth are woven into the story of the Nation, without defensiveness and without denial.

For scholars, students, and general readers who care about how race and capitalism have worked in North America and who are willing to follow the money into places that do not fit neat Black and white, North and South frames.

If you come from one of these groups, you will see your usual lane here, and you will also see beyond it.

How to Read This Book

You do not have to read this book like a textbook.

If you want a narrative, you can move from Part I through Part V and treat it as a long story.

If you are interested in policy, you may want to pay special attention to the chapters on the Treaty of 1866, the Outlet, allotment, and Greenwood, then read the timeline and glossary.

If you are interested in family history, you may want to read the case studies and the atlas, then use the notes and appendices as a guide for your own document hunts.

However, you move through it, keep the four questions in mind.

Who created the value.
Who recorded it.
Who captured it.
Who was written out.

The answers change from scene to scene. The pattern does not.

That is why a ledger tells the truth. It is hard to argue with what you can count, especially when you finally put the missing names back on the page.

CHAPTER 1

Slavery in the Cherokee Nation: An Economic System

On paper, it looks simple.

A name.
A column for "slaves."
A number.

In the 1835 census, one Cherokee household might be listed with two enslaved people, another with twenty, most with none at all. On the page, the enslaved people are weightless. They take up no more space than a tick mark.

Outside those pages, their work was heavy.

They cleared fields, lifted beams, planted crops, mended fences, fired bricks, rowed ferries, cooked meals, spun thread, and watched children. They built houses that still stand. They laid the economic foundation for a small group of wealthy Cherokee families, and for a national economy that began to look more and more like the plantation South.

If you look only at the moral story, all of that can blur together as "slavery."

If you look at it as a system for creating and capturing value, a different picture comes into focus.

This chapter lays out that system. It does not try to cover every detail of Cherokee slavery. It does something more basic and less comfortable. It treats slavery in the Cherokee Nation as an economic machine, then asks where the power and the profits went.

From Captives to Capital

Slavery among Cherokees did not start as a full copy of Southern plantation slavery.

For a long time, Cherokees, like other Native nations, practiced forms of captivity. People taken in war might be killed, adopted into families, or held as captives in ways that blended punishment, replacement of lost kin, and political control. Captivity was harsh, but it still sat inside a kinship-based world.

As European colonies expanded in the Southeast, as traders came in and out, and as plantation agriculture spread, a different model arrived. Africans and people of African descent were treated, in law and in markets, as property. Their status passed by the mother. Their labor and their children could be bought and sold.

Over the late eighteenth and early nineteenth centuries, elite Cherokees began to take up this system. They bought African and African American slaves from nearby markets. They sometimes married white traders or took on white family ties. They raised cash crops for sale. They passed both land and enslaved people down as property in wills.

By the early 1800s, what had been a kinship-based practice of captivity in some Cherokee communities was giving way to a race based, market driven form of slavery.

That shift did not happen evenly or all at once. Many Cherokees never owned an enslaved person. Some opposed the new system. Others held on to older practices longer. But by the time the United States began to push hard for removal, a small group of slaveholding Cherokee families held a disproportionate share of the Nation's wealth.

The ledgers show it.

Counting the Slaveholding Class

In 1809, a federal agent counted 583 enslaved people in the Cherokee Nation and put a dollar value on them. In the same records, a single wealthy Cherokee, James Vann, appears with well over one hundred enslaved people on his land. He held close to a fifth of all enslaved people in the Nation at the time.

By 1835, on the eve of removal, federal census takers counted roughly 1,600 enslaved people among the Cherokees. The number of Cherokee households that held those people was small. Historians working from the same sources estimate that slaveholding households made up around 6 to 7 percent of all Cherokee households.

So fewer than one in ten households held enslaved people.

On its face, that might sound almost minor. In the ledger, it is not minor at all.

When researchers reconstruct acreage from that 1835 snapshot, a stark pattern appears. Slaveholders farmed on average several times more land than non-slaveholders. The gap is often summarized as something like this:

- slaveholding households cultivating in the range of seventy or more acres on average

- non-slaveholding households cultivating around ten acres on average

The exact number shifts from source to source, but the structure is steady. A small minority of slaveholding families controlled a large share of the improved land.

Put simply, enslaved labor allowed those families to expand their land use, produce more crops, and enter markets that most other Cherokees could not touch on the same scale.

In the ledger language of this book:

- Enslaved Black people **created** a large portion of the Nation's agricultural value.

- Planter households **recorded** that value in their own names, in farm reports, estate inventories, and loan papers.

- Those same households **captured** most of the income and long-term wealth that flowed from that labor.

- The people doing the work were usually **written out** of the accounts, named only as "boy," "girl," "woman," "man," or as a first name next to a dollar figure.

What Enslaved Labor Actually Did

It is easy to say "slavery supported agriculture" and leave it there. The work itself deserves more detail.

Enslaved Black people in the Cherokee Nation did at least four broad kinds of work that mattered for wealth:

1. **Field labor**

2. **Household and care work**

3. **Skilled and semi-skilled trades**

4. **Service and transport**

1. Field labor

On Cherokee plantations and larger farms in the East, enslaved men, women, and children cleared forest, broke new ground, planted and harvested crops, and tended livestock.

Corn and livestock formed the base of the food supply. Cotton and other cash crops tied Cherokee planters into regional and international markets.

Clearing land in this context was not a onetime act. Trees had to be cut, stumps removed, brush burned, soil prepared, fences built and repaired, fields weeded and re planted year after year. Each acre moved from forest to field represented hundreds of hours of human labor, most of it unpaid.

The more enslaved people a household held, the more land it could bring under cultivation. The more land it worked, the more crops it could raise for sale, and the more surplus it could turn into cash, livestock, tools, and buildings.

From a ledger standpoint, enslaved people increased both the productive capacity of the land and the speed at which a family could move from subsistence to surplus.

2. Household and care work

Enslaved women and girls often carried the bulk of domestic labor. Cooking, cleaning, spinning, weaving, nursing infants, caring for sick family members, tending gardens, carrying water, and making clothing all fell within this sphere.

This work rarely shows up in farm reports or account books in a direct way. It shows up indirectly, in the time and energy freed up for slaveholding Cherokees to focus on public politics, commercial ventures, and the visible side of "progress."

In many Cherokee communities, women had long been central to agriculture and property control. As plantation style slavery expanded, gender roles shifted. Men increasingly stepped into the role of plantation masters and farm managers, while the domestic sphere, always important, became more tightly tied to enslaved women's work.

The wealth that emerged from this arrangement rested on both visible field labor and hidden household labor, nearly all of it done by Black people whose names we know only in fragments.

3. Skilled and semi-skilled trades

Not all enslaved work was in fields or kitchens.

Brickmaking, blacksmithing, carpentry, mill work, and other skilled trades depended heavily on Black labor. When you stand in front of a brick mansion built by a slaveholding Cherokee or in front of the ruins of a public building from that era, you are looking at work that almost certainly ran through Black hands.

Brick kilns required long hours and precise work. Mills and stills required technical skill and maintenance. Ferries and roads required engineering and constant repair. In each case, Cherokee elites could convert enslaved labor into higher value services and products, not just raw crops.

4. Service and transport

Ferries, inns, taverns, and toll roads appear again and again in records of wealthy Cherokee families. These businesses sat on key routes, including the Federal Road pushed through Cherokee country with federal support.

Enslaved labor powered these services. Black workers rowed the ferries, cared for horses, carried luggage, cooked and served food, cleaned rooms, and handled travelers' needs. The profits from these businesses went primarily to their Cherokee owners, but the daily work that kept them running came from enslaved people whose legal status prevented them from capturing the same gains.

Taken together, these forms of labor made Black chattel slavery far more than a domestic institution. It was a central engine of investment and diversification in the Cherokee economy.

People as Capital

In the emerging Cherokee planter economy, enslaved Black people were treated not only as a labor force, but as capital.

They could be taxed as property. They could be mortgaged, hired out, and seized to satisfy debts. They could be inherited and divided as part of an estate.

Account books, probate files, and court records show this clearly.

A sheriff's sale might list "one Negro man named Peter" to be sold to satisfy a judgment. An estate inventory might group "three negroes, Joe, his wife Nelly and child" with livestock and tools to be auctioned on credit. A reward notice for a runaway might offer one hundred dollars for the capture and return of "a likely mulatto man," a sum that signals both his value as labor and his owner's expectation of recapturing that value.

The Cherokee Nation itself, through statutes and courts, participated in this system. Legislative acts defined enslaved people as property, set rules for their discipline and sale, and, at times, punished those who helped them run away. The national government did not own enslaved people as a corporate body, but it supported and protected the property claims of citizens who did.

For slaveholding Cherokees, this meant that wealth could be built and defended across generations through both land and people. Land could be improved with enslaved labor. Enslaved people themselves could be pledged as security on loans. Children born to enslaved women added to the owner's asset column.

For enslaved Black people, it meant that their bodies and their families were tied to the financial fortunes of their owners in ways that reduced human life to entries on a balance sheet.

In later chapters, when we look at how Cherokee law defined citizenship and ownership, this early treatment of humans as capital will matter. It shaped who had the power to buy land, who had the credit to withstand shocks, and who entered the allotment era with existing assets versus only potential labor.

Class, Color, and the Shape of "Progress"

The adoption of plantation style slavery did not just increase production. It changed Cherokee society from the inside.

A small planter class emerged, made up largely of families with mixed Cherokee and white ancestry, strong ties to external markets, and access to both land and credit. They built larger houses, sent children to mission schools, held key political offices, and sat at the center of debates over removal, law, and national direction.

Most Cherokees did not own slaves. Many lived on smaller farms, raised food for their families, and participated in local trade without large surpluses. Some owned no improved land at all.

The gap between the slaveholding minority and the majority showed up in:

- land under cultivation

- number of livestock

- access to outside markets

- influence in national politics

In this period, certain laws also drew tighter racial lines. Statutes against "amalgamation" with Black people, restrictions on the status of mixed African and Cherokee children, and rules that tied Blackness to enslavement reinforced the planter class's belief in a racial hierarchy that justified their economic position.

At the same time, African and Cherokee people influenced one another in daily life. In fields and kitchens, in gardens and sickrooms, knowledge moved both ways: agricultural practices, food, herbal medicine, and craft skills crossed boundaries even as law tried to harden them.

From the ledger perspective, the key point is this.

Class and race became linked in new ways. The households that benefited most from slavery tended to be lighter skinned, more connected to white relatives and traders, and more involved in national politics. Enslaved Black people and poor non-slaveholding Cherokees often lived close to one another in material terms, but the law treated them very differently.

When removal came, that distinction would matter.

Removal as a Stress Test

The system described so far rested on three things:

- land in the eastern homelands

- enslaved labor to work that land and diversify businesses

- political structures that protected slaveholders' property claims

Forced removal put all three under strain.

When the United States forced Cherokees west in the late 1830s, it insisted that the Treaty of New Echota cleared title to Cherokee land in the East. Houses, barns, mills, and cleared fields were left behind. Some families received compensation on paper for improvements, often at reduced values. Others did not.

Enslaved people did not stay behind. Owners brought many of them west, on roads where Black labor again did critical work: cutting paths, driving teams, cooking, guarding, and caring for ill children and elders.

The asset side of the ledger changed shape.

For slaveholders, land was stripped from the balance sheet or reduced to uncertain claims for compensation. Enslaved people remained as mobile capital. In the West, they would be used again to clear land, rebuild homes, and restart agriculture.

For enslaved Black people, removal compounded loss. They were uprooted along with their owners, separated from familiar terrain and networks, and assigned to build a new economy that they would still not control.

From the Nation's point of view, the removal era exposed how deeply the economy depended on unfree labor. As soon as the Nation began to rebuild in Indian Territory, slaveholding families leaned heavily on enslaved Black people to rebuild their farms, mills, and businesses. We will see that in detail in the next chapter.

For now, it is enough to note that slavery was not just a pre-removal phenomenon to be left behind with Georgia fields. It migrated west. It was baked into the early economic structure of the Cherokee Nation in Indian Territory.

The Ledger at the End of the Chapter

If we were to sketch a rough ledger for slavery in the Cherokee Nation before removal, it might look like this.

Value created

- Fields cleared and expanded

- Corn, cotton, and livestock raised for sale

- Houses, mills, ferries, taverns, and roads built and operated

- Skills developed in agriculture, construction, and crafts

Almost all of this value came from the labor of enslaved Black people, alongside the work of non-slaveholding Cherokees and others.

Value recorded

- Census counts of farms, houses, and enslaved people

- Estate inventories listing enslaved people, land, and improvements

- Court records, bills of sale, reward notices, and tax lists

Most of these records list slaveholding Cherokees as the owners and decision makers.

Value captured

- Land ownership concentrated in a small slaveholding class

- Cash income from crops, rents, and hired out labor

- Ownership of businesses along key roads and rivers

- Political power in national councils and treaty negotiations

The people who benefited most were the families who held land and enslaved people together.

Value lost or redirected

- Enslaved Black people lost control over their own labor, families, and movement.

- Non-slaveholding Cherokees found themselves increasingly at a disadvantage in land and market access.

- As removal approached, Eastern improvements were lost or underpaid, with the gains from that loss flowing largely to white states and settlers.

Seeing this clearly does not answer every moral or political question. It does something more basic. It tells us that slavery in the Cherokee Nation was not an aside or an uncomfortable detail. It was a central part of how wealth was created, counted, and defended.

In the next chapter, we look more closely at how people themselves appear as property in the records and what that meant for both the enslaved and their owners when the time came to move west.

CHAPTER 2

People as Property: How Wealth Was Measured

When you look at the early nineteenth century reports on the Cherokee Nation, you do not just see people. You see columns.

Houses.
Cattle.
Horses.
Mills.
Enslaved "Negroes."

In 1809, a federal agent listed the Nation's wealth in neat rows. He counted more than twelve thousand Cherokees, hundreds of whites living among them, and 583 enslaved Black people. He also listed thousands of cattle, horses, sheep, and the value of improvements such as mills and ploughs. Slaves were set out with a national total and an average value per person.

On that page, an enslaved man or woman appears in the same kind of line as a cow or a house. Each is an "item" with a price. Each contributes to the total worth of the Nation.

That is what this chapter is about.

How the system turned human beings into capital on the books. How those numbers shaped who looked rich, who counted as respectable, and who had leverage when the ground shifted under everyone's feet.

The National Balance Sheet

The 1809 survey was not a private planter's notebook. It was a governmental snapshot. Officials wanted to know what the Cherokee Nation looked like in numbers.

They counted:

- Cherokee people

- "Negro slaves"

- white residents

- livestock

- cultivated land

- mills and other improvements

Alongside that head count, they estimated the value of property in dollars. One table from later work with the same census shows enslaved people grouped as "583 negro slaves" with an average valuation of several hundred dollars each, forming a large share of the total wealth column for the Nation.

A simple comparison runs through the secondary literature. In these records, the average enslaved person is valued many times higher than a basic log house. A human body with years of labor ahead of it appears as a more valuable "asset" than the structure that shelters a family.

By 1835, another federal census again counted enslaved people alongside land, livestock, and other property. The number of enslaved Black people had nearly tripled since 1809. Slaveholding households still made up a small portion of all Cherokee households, roughly in the single digits of total families, but their share of wealth was far larger.

On these balance sheets, enslaved people did several jobs at once.

They stood for the potential labor a planter could command. They served as visible proof of status. They were treated as collateral that could be taxed, mortgaged, or seized.

The ledgers did not ask who they were. The ledgers asked what they were worth.

Property on Paper, Flesh in Practice

When enslaved people appear in court files and estate papers from this period, they are usually presented in three tight clusters of information:

- name, often only a first name

- age or a rough description such as "boy," "girl," "woman," "man"

- a dollar amount

"George, aged about twenty-five, valued at three hundred dollars." "Mary and her three children, sold together for nine hundred dollars."

Sometimes the records do not bother with a name at all. They speak of "one likely negro boy" or "a negro man named Peter," identified just enough for a sheriff to sell him at public auction to satisfy a judgment.

These entries show how law, markets, and everyday practice wrapped around each other.

- The national government allowed and regulated slavery through statutes and courts.

- Cherokee marshals and sheriffs enforced property rights that included rights in human beings.

- Creditors treated enslaved people as assets that could be used to pay off debts.

Every time a court ordered an auction that included enslaved people, the economic system made a clear statement.

A human life could be converted into cash on demand.

Debt and default did not just threaten land. They threatened families. A planter who had pledged both land and people as security might keep his fields while losing the people whose labor made those fields productive. Or the land might go and the enslaved people remain, now owned by someone else, their personal lives reorganized to answer new needs.

Tax Rolls and Chattel

Another place enslaved people show up is in tax lists and local assessments.

Slaveholding Cherokee citizens could be taxed on their enslaved "property" as well as on land, livestock, and mills. The exact rules changed over time, but the basic principle held. Enslaved people were part of the taxable base that supported the national government.

This had at least three effects.

First, it made slaveholding itself a marker of being part of the economic elite. Only those with enough resources to own taxable human property could claim that status.

Second, it tied the fortunes of the national treasury to the fortunes of the planter class. When planters prospered, tax receipts rose. When they suffered, the treasury felt it.

Third, it hardened the idea that enslaved Black people existed inside Cherokee law primarily as property. Their presence in tax lists focused on their cash value, not their personhood.

From the ledger perspective, enslaved people functioned in these lists as a kind of reserve wealth. They did not just generate value through work. They stood, in the eyes of the state, as portable value that could be counted and, if needed, converted into money.

Collateral and Credit

The treatment of enslaved people as chattel property made them central to the credit system of the Nation.

If a wealthy Cherokee wanted to borrow money, he could offer a mix of assets as security. Land, buildings, livestock, and enslaved people could all be named in a mortgage, bond, or note.

Records from estate sales and debt cases show how this worked.

A court might order that "one negro man named Gabriel" be sold to satisfy a 500-dollar judgment. A mortgage might be settled by transferring "one boy named Grigg" from one owner to another as payment. Families such as the Vanns, Ridges, and Rosses feature repeatedly in documents where enslaved people were counted as part of complex webs of debt and obligation.

In this world, enslaved people were a kind of living bank. Owners could:

- hire them out and collect wages

- lease them with land as a package

- pledge them as collateral

- sell them outright to raise cash

The enslaved did not benefit from any of this financial flexibility. They experienced it as a constant insecurity. A change in an owner's finances could mean sale, forced migration, or the breakup of families.

For non-slaveholding Cherokees, the growing reliance on this kind of collateral meant something else. It meant that those without human property had less access to big loans and commercial partnerships. Their land and labor mattered, but they had fewer assets the courts and creditors treated as high value security.

Over time, this widened the gap between slaveholding families and others, even within the same Nation and often the same communities.

Human Capital and National Wealth

The 1809 and 1835 snapshots together tell us that the number of enslaved people in the Cherokee Nation grew from the hundreds into the low thousands in the space of a few decades.

To understand what that meant for wealth, it helps to look at how those same reports and later analyses valued property.

In table form, one influential reconstruction of the 1835 census lists:

- cultivated land and houses with certain dollar values

- livestock with others

- "583 negro slaves @ average 300 dollars" multiplied out in an earlier estimate of national wealth

In other words:

- a log house might be valued at a few tens of dollars

- an enslaved person at several hundred

Without getting lost in exact figures, the relative scale matters.

In pure accounting terms, a single enslaved person could equal multiple modest houses. A group of ten or twenty could represent the core of an estate's value. That kind of "human capital" made slaveholders look very rich on paper even before you counted the crops produced by enslaved labor.

That value was not abstract. It could be inherited, divided in wills, and used to support younger generations. Children of slaveholders could be launched into adulthood with already existing assets behind them.

For enslaved Black people, that same valuation meant that every child born to an enslaved mother added to someone else's wealth line. The new life appeared first as a number in someone's property ledger, not as a person with a claim to the fruits of their own future labor.

Buying Freedom, Using the System

Within this harsh system, there are a few recorded moments when enslaved people managed to use Cherokee law to carve out a different outcome.

Court dockets, petitions, and later testimonies include cases of enslaved men and women who raised money and bought their own freedom through formal transactions.

An enslaved man might appear in a court record paying a lump sum for his liberty, backed by years of savings from hired out labor. A woman might use her knowledge of the law and her owner's debts to negotiate a price for herself and her children.

The details are sparse, but the pattern is clear.

Even in a regime that classified them as property, Black people studied the rules, found openings, and sometimes used the very tools that oppressed them to alter their status. They turned wages, favors, and relationships into cash and then into manumission.

These cases did not overturn the system. They show that enslaved people were not just acted upon. They acted, thought, and calculated in a world that tried to define them only as numbers.

From the ledger side, a man buying his own freedom looks like one asset moving off the owner's books. From the human side, it is a person stepping across a line that never should have existed in the first place.

The Moral Fog of "Progress"

For slaveholding Cherokees who embraced plantation agriculture, owning enslaved people became part of a self-image that mixed economic ambition, a desire for security, and a hunger for recognition in a white dominated world.

Editorials and speeches from the era show some leaders defending slavery as proof that Cherokees had become "civilized" in the eyes of the United States. Newspaper editors argued that the Nation's embrace of plantation style agriculture, permanent houses, and schools showed readiness for equal treatment. Some made the case that owning Black slaves put Cherokees on the same economic footing as their white neighbors.

Inside that moral fog, a painful equation took hold.

To look respectable and modern was to look like a southern planter.
To look like a southern planter required land and Black chattel. To hold onto land in the face of American pressure seemed to require meeting American expectations of "improvement."

The cost of that bargain fell on enslaved Black people and on the social fabric of the Nation itself. A small number of families accumulated more land and capital, while the majority of Cherokees watched class lines sharpen and racial categories harden in ways that echoed the very society pushing them off their homelands.

Preparing for the Shock

By the time federal troops and state militias began to force Cherokees into stockades in 1838, the economic system was set.

A small number of slaveholding families held disproportionate wealth in:

- land under cultivation

- livestock

- mills, ferries, taverns, and roads

- enslaved Black people treated as capital

Most Cherokees did not have those same reserves.

From the ledger angle, the removal crisis was about more than land loss. It was a test of what counted as wealth that could survive movement and what could not.

- Land, houses, and fixed improvements were vulnerable.

- Livestock could be driven but not always with enough feed or care.

- Paper claims for compensation might or might not be honored.

- Enslaved people could be moved, guarded, and worked in a new place.

Cherokee leaders knew this. They argued over treaties and strategies in public, but they also made private calculations about how to preserve family fortunes in a time of upheaval.

Enslaved Black people, already treated as property on paper, were central to those calculations. The very fact that they could walk and work made them, in the cold logic of the moment, one of the few "assets" that owners expected to carry intact into the West.

That is where Chapter 3 begins.

There we look at removal itself as a form of asset destruction and transfer. We follow the fields, houses, and improvements left behind, the bodies forced west, and the way the old balance sheet fell apart and reassembled around a new land base in Indian Territory.

CHAPTER 3

Removal as Asset Destruction

Imagine walking past a Cherokee farm in North Georgia in the fall of 1838 after the soldiers have done their work.

The house is still standing. Corn still hangs from the rafters. Fences still hold their shape. The orchard still makes shade.

The family is gone.

In a matter of weeks, what had been the fixed base of one household's wealth becomes an open invitation. A white neighbor, a speculator, a man with a state land lottery ticket, can step in and claim it. The structures do not move. The people do. The wealth follows the structures, not the people.

This is what removal looks like when you treat it not just as a tragedy, but as an economic event. It is an act of asset destruction and asset transfer at scale.

The Day the Ledger Froze

Long before soldiers showed up at Cherokee doors, commissioners and valuing agents had already started to turn farms into numbers.

Under the terms that followed the Treaty of New Echota, federal agents came into the Nation to record "improvements" and assign dollar amounts to cabins, fields, orchards, ferries, mills, and other property. They also recorded livestock and certain forms of personal property. In theory, this paper trail would be used to pay Cherokees for what they left behind when they moved west.

In practice, the process was uneven and often biased downward.

Some farms were never fully assessed. Some valuations were obviously too low. Some families simply did not trust the process or refused to sign off.

The 1838 claims that Cherokees filed just before forced removal show how dissatisfied people were. Thousands of petitions poured in, asking for corrections or new valuations. Men and women listed:

- houses

- smokehouses

- corncribs

- fences

- peach and apple trees

- livestock

- ferry rights

- mills

and argued that government agents had undervalued or ignored them.

That rush of claims did not stop the soldiers. It did something else. It froze the ledger.

On paper, the United States now held a snapshot of Cherokee property in the East, labeled and priced. Once the deadline for claims passed, anything not written down might as well not exist.

Removal then turned that frozen picture into a one-sided exchange.

Treaty Math

The legal basis for that exchange was the Treaty of New Echota, signed in 1835 by a small group of Cherokees and used by the United States as if the whole Nation had agreed.

Under that treaty, the Cherokee Nation ceded all its lands east of the Mississippi River and "all their lands and possessions" there to the United States. In return, the United States promised a block of land in Indian Territory, money, and certain forms of assistance.

The treaty set a headline number:

- up to five million dollars for all lands and possessions east of the Mississippi

It also left room for an additional three hundred thousand dollars if the Senate decided that spoliation claims had not been covered.

On state maps, the land being surrendered is often described as roughly seven million acres spread across Georgia, Alabama, Tennessee, and North Carolina.

If you do the rough math, five million dollars for seven million acres comes out to well under a dollar an acre, before you even count the value of buildings, fences, orchards, ferries, and mills.

Economic historians who have reworked these numbers with better land price data reach a clear conclusion. The largest cost borne by the Cherokees was not the physical move west, and not even the loss of one season's crops. It was the uncompensated value of the land itself, followed by the lost agricultural output that land would have produced in the years after removal.

In other words, the treaty math already assumed an enormous discount on what Cherokee land and improvements were actually worth. The claims process that followed often pushed values even lower.

From the ledger side, the United States acquired millions of acres and the improvements on them at a bargain price. White settlers and states would reap that gain in later years through cotton, timber, mining, and town building.

What Was Left Behind

To understand removal as asset destruction, it helps to list what was actually left on the ground when Cherokees were marched away.

- Houses and cabins

- Barns, smokehouses, and corncribs

- Fences stretching across hillsides

- Cleared fields and pastures

- Orchards that took years to mature

- Mills on rivers and streams

- Ferries and rights of way

- Churches and community buildings

All of these were fixed assets. You could not carry a cabin on your back. You could not uproot a full-grown peach orchard and put it on a wagon. You could not roll up a millpond and move it to Indian Territory.

The federal removal program promised that Cherokees would be paid for these things, either through the treaty's lump sum, through individual claims, or through later boards of commissioners. Some people did receive payments or credits. Many did not receive anything close to what they lost.

On the ground, something else happened.

Once Cherokees were gone, their houses, fields, and orchards became available to others. State land lotteries and informal occupation allowed white families to move into abandoned Cherokee homes or build on the same foundations. Rivers and roads that

Cherokees had built their lives around now served new owners with no obligation to repay the people who had done the work.

In economic terms, removal turned:

- Cherokee fixed capital in the East

- into white fixed capital in the same place

with only partial, delayed, or entirely missing compensation to the original owners.

Who and What Could Move

Not all assets were fixed. Some things could travel.

- People

- Livestock

- Portable tools and household goods

- Paper claims

When federal troops and state militias began rounding up Cherokees in 1838, they herded families into stockades and camps before sending them west in organized detachments. Estimates vary, but roughly sixteen thousand Cherokees were forced west in 1838 and 1839.

They did not travel alone.

Accounts from the time and later studies agree that more than a thousand enslaved Black people, often counted at around sixteen hundred, accompanied Cherokee slaveholders on the Trail.

For slaveholding Cherokees, this meant that some of their most valuable "property" could be taken along. Enslaved Black men, women, and children walked beside or behind Cherokee families, guarded by soldiers, performing much of the work that made the march possible.

On the road, enslaved people:

- cleared obstructions from the path

- hunted and cooked

- tended animals

- carried supplies

- watched children and the elderly

They were still counted as property, even as they did the labor that kept entire detachments alive.

Livestock could move too, but with higher risk. Cattle and hogs might be driven, but hunger, theft, and disease cut into those numbers. Horses and mules were valuable but could be lost or stolen on the way. Tools and household items could be packed into wagons or carried, but there was only so much space and strength.

Paper claims could travel easily enough. Their problem was not weight. Their problem was enforcement.

Death as Economic Loss

When people talk about the Trail of Tears, they often quote a simple figure. Four thousand Cherokees died during removal.

Modern economic work has tried to refine that number, sometimes estimating a somewhat lower direct death toll. What has not changed is the basic reality. Thousands of Cherokees died in stockades and along the routes west because of disease, exposure, and hardship.

Every death was a human loss first.

From an economic angle, those deaths also represented destroyed human capital:

- farmers who would never plant again

- women who would never transmit skills and knowledge

- children whose future labor and creativity were cut off

- community leaders, translators, and artisans whose capacity could not be replaced quickly

For families already stripped of fixed assets in the East, the death of a parent or child was a second blow. They reached Indian Territory with fewer working hands and more grief, and had to start over on new land that was unfamiliar and often less productive in the short term.

Enslaved people died too. Their deaths do not show up as loudly in white or federal records, but they lived under the same exposure and disease, on rations and in conditions that were often worse. Owners might record the loss of "a negro girl" or "a boy" as a reduction in property, but the human loss for Black families was just as deep.

Transfer, Not Just Destruction

It is tempting to think of removal mostly as pure loss for the Cherokees and pure gain for the United States. The truth is more complicated on both sides, but the flow of assets is clear.

Economic studies that model the costs of removal compare:

- the value of land and improvements in the East

- the costs of moving people and some property west

- the value of the land received in Indian Territory

- the adjustment period after resettlement

They find that the biggest hit to the Cherokee side of the ledger came from the gap between what the land and improvements in the East were worth and what they were actually paid. The second biggest hit came from lost agricultural output during and right after removal.

On the American side, taxpayers covered some removal costs in cash, food, and military logistics. But the states and private citizens who took over former Cherokee land stood to profit for generations.

Cotton brought money in. Timber went out. Gold and other minerals came up out of the ground. Towns grew where Cherokee towns had been.

From the point of view of white Georgia, Alabama, and other states, removal was a massive transfer of productive capacity into their hands. The degraded payments to Cherokees were a cost of doing business, not a true market price.

Unequal Starting Lines in Indian Territory

When Cherokees and the people enslaved by them reached Indian Territory, they did not all start from the same place.

Families that had owned land, livestock, and especially enslaved people often brought:

- some cash or treaty money

- wagons and tools

- herds, if they survived

- the continued ability to command Black labor without pay

Non-slaveholding Cherokees typically arrived with much less:

- some personal goods

- perhaps a few animals

- skills and knowledge, but few movable assets

Enslaved Black people arrived with their bodies, their skills, and any small personal belongings they could keep from seizure or loss. Legally, they were still property of their Cherokee owners. They did not control land. They did not receive treaty payments in their own names.

So, removal did not level the field. It often widened existing gaps.

The planter class, hit hard by the loss of Eastern estates, still had more capital with which to rebuild. They could again use enslaved labor to:

- clear new land

- build new houses

- plant large fields

- start new businesses along rivers and roads

In later decades, they would appear in the records of Indian Territory as major landowners, merchants, and political leaders. The fact that their wealth had survived through removal rested heavily on one thing. They had been allowed to carry key assets west, including the people they enslaved.

Non-slaveholding Cherokees and enslaved Black people had to climb a steeper hill. They worked the same ground, under the same sun, but with far fewer tools and claims.

The Removal Ledger

If we put the removal years into the same fourfold ledger used throughout this book, it looks like this.

Value destroyed

- Cherokee ownership of millions of acres in the East

- houses, barns, mills, and orchards left behind or taken without full payment

- human lives lost on the road and in camps

- years of agricultural output during the transition

Value transferred

- Eastern land and improvements into state and private hands in the Southeast

- control of roads, ferries, and town sites to white counties and towns

- long term land rents, crop profits, and mineral wealth to non-Cherokee owners

Value carried

- enslaved Black people moved west as capital and labor

- some livestock, tools, and household goods

- treaty funds and claims, often underpaid, sometimes still usable

- political experience and institutional knowledge

Value reassembled

- in Indian Territory, slaveholders rebuilt wealth by using enslaved labor on new land

- non-slaveholding Cherokees tried to restore household economies with less capital

- enslaved Black people continued to generate value they did not capture, now on a new land base

Seeing removal this way does not reduce it to numbers. It makes clear that those numbers and the assets behind them shaped who could rebuild and who could not.

In the next chapter we watch that rebuilding begins. We look closely at how the Nation used enslaved labor to reconstruct its economy in Indian Territory and how the same system that had fueled plantation wealth in the East was redeployed to raise new houses, fences, and fields in the West.

CHAPTER 4

Forced Reconstruction in Indian Territory

By the time the last Cherokee detachments reached Indian Territory, the old balance sheet was gone.

The houses, orchards, and mills that had anchored wealth in Georgia and North Carolina were behind them. The claims they had filed on those improvements were folded into federal files, out of reach. The new land promised in treaty text was real enough, but it was mostly trees, grass, and creek bottom. There were few fences. Few houses. No long-standing roads.

The Nation had to rebuild from almost nothing.

The question was who would do the work, and who would own the result.

A Nation Replanted

In 1839, Cherokees adopted a new constitution in the West and selected a capital at Tahlequah. They reestablished a national council, courts, and executive offices. They mapped districts and held elections. All of that looks political on the surface. Underneath, it was economic.

A capital needed buildings.

A government needed roads to reach it.

Courts needed a house.

Councils needed a meeting hall.

Officials needed houses and farms to support them.

Beyond the town site, families needed cabins, fenced fields, barns, smokehouses, and mills. Churches and schools would come later, but the first years were about survival and basic structure.

The land in Indian Territory was not empty. It had long been home to other Native nations and local communities. But for Cherokees freshly arrived from the East, it was a new grid to carve. They had to:

- choose where to settle

- clear timber

- break prairie and bottom land

- stake out roads and crossings

And they had to do it while dealing with disease, internal political conflict, and the memory of the Trail.

In that setting, the same group that had held advantage in the East still held a crucial edge. Slaveholding families had more movable capital, more livestock, and, most importantly, control over enslaved Black labor. That gave them a faster path back to something like the life they had lost.

Building a New Capital on Old Labor

Tahlequah did not appear out of thin air. It rose out of work.

When the Nation decided to fix its capital there, they had to raise:

- a council house

- a supreme court building

- offices for national officers

- storage for records and supplies

Later they would add seminaries for education, mission schools, and other public buildings.

There is no single master list that names every hand that laid every brick or sawed every board. But the pattern of the time, and the surviving records, make one thing clear. Enslaved Black men did a great deal of the heavy and skilled labor.

The same mix of work that had built planter houses and public buildings in the East reappeared in the West:

- felling and hauling timber

- digging foundations

- firing bricks and laying them

- mixing mortar

- cutting stone

- raising frames

Slaveholding Cherokee officials and contractors brought enslaved workers onto public building sites. In some cases, they were paid for the hire of those workers from public funds. In other cases, they simply drew on privately held labor to meet public needs.

From the ledger perspective, that meant:

- the Nation as a whole benefited from new public buildings raised quickly

- the planter class captured additional value by turning enslaved labor into wages or influence

- enslaved Black people, again, created value they could not own or pass down

The Supreme Court building, the council house, and early seminaries in Indian Territory did not float above this system. They sat on top of it.

Clearing, Fencing, and Planting the West

Outside the capital, the work of reconstruction looked like this.

Crews of enslaved men, often under the direction of Cherokee owners, cut into the forest and prairie. They cleared brush, felled large trees, burned stumps, and dragged rocks out of future fields. They fenced off parcels, dug wells, and planted corn, beans, and fruit trees.

Enslaved women and children joined in planting, weeding, and harvest, then took on the same domestic and care work they had done in the East.

Each farm they helped establish became another node in the new Cherokee economy.

For slaveholding families, the arrangement meant that:

- they could bring more land into cultivation more quickly

- they could build larger houses and barns sooner

- they could raise surplus crops for sale or trade

Non-slaveholding Cherokees also cleared land and built farms, but they did so with fewer hands, often relying on family labor and modest mutual aid. Their pace was slower. Their early fields were smaller. Their ability to build surplus, and therefore wealth, lagged behind.

The gap that had opened in the East between a small planter class and the rest of the Nation thus reappeared in the West, this time on new ground.

Removal had cut off the old fixed assets, but it had not eliminated the unequal distribution of mobile capital. To the contrary, the same unequal distribution shaped how quickly households could transform "raw" Indian Territory land into productive farms and ranches.

Salt, Mills, and Other Engines

Agriculture was only one part of the reconstruction. Cherokee leaders and entrepreneurs also turned again to industries that had been profitable in the East: mills, salt works, and trade routes.

Salt springs in the West, like those in the East, were valuable communal resources. The Nation could lease them to individuals or companies, who then used enslaved labor to extract salt and sell it to neighboring communities.

Gristmills and sawmills went up along creeks and rivers. These mills processed local grain and timber, turning subsistence harvests into saleable flour and boards. Their owners, often the same slaveholding families who had held capital in the East, used enslaved labor to run the wheels and maintain the equipment.

Ferries across rivers and wagon roads into neighboring lands needed constant upkeep. Once again, it was enslaved Black workers who did much of the physical work, while Cherokee owners collected tolls and fees.

From the ledger side:

- the value of salt, milling, and transport services in Indian Territory arose from the combination of a communal resource (springs, streams, roads) and unfree labor

- profits went mainly to those with the capital to lease sites and purchase enslaved people

- the Nation benefited as a political unit from having these services, but did not distribute their gains equally among citizens

These industries also tied the Nation back into regional trade networks, linking Cherokee communities in Indian Territory to markets in Arkansas, Missouri, Kansas, and Texas. That connection would matter later, when Civil War and federal policy turned the region into a battleground again.

Law in the New Land

As the Nation rebuilt its physical plant, it also rebuilt its legal system.

The 1839 constitution in Indian Territory reaffirmed Cherokee sovereignty and set out the structure of government. It also, by silence and by statute, continued to recognize Black chattel slavery.

Early western laws addressed:

- the status of enslaved people

- punishment for runaways and for those who helped them

- rights of slaveholders to move and control their "property"

- taxes and regulations on slaveholding

These laws did not invent slavery in the West. They carried the Eastern system forward into the new geography.

At the same time, political changes were reshaping who held power.

The new western government centralized authority in a national council and executive. Voting rights and office holding were tied to male heads of household. Women, who had once held strong positions in matrilineal clans and community governance, found their formal political role diminished. The same planter class that had benefited from slavery in the East now helped write the rules in the West. Many of them were slaveholders.

This matters for the ledger because it meant:

- the people who wrote the economic and legal rules were often the same people who had the most to gain from preserving slavery

- Black Cherokees and enslaved people had little direct input into law, even though their labor was central to the Nation's material reconstruction

The gap between who built the country and who wrote its rules widened.

Resistance and Fear

Enslaved people did not accept this situation quietly.

Tentative and overt acts of resistance appeared in the new land as they had in the old:

- running away to nearby Native, Black, or mixed communities

- slowing work or damaging tools

- negotiating for better treatment or, in rare cases, for freedom

One large scale episode, an 1842 revolt by enslaved people in the Cherokee Nation who attempted to escape south, terrified slaveholding citizens and underscored the instability of a system that depended on forced labor.

In response, some Cherokees hardened their pro-slavery stance. Patrollers and legal penalties intensified. Others began to question whether the risks and moral costs of slavery were worth the apparent economic gains. Internal debates sharpened, especially as missionary voices and some traditional leaders raised objections.

From the economic angle, this tension meant that the very labor force the Nation was relying on to rebuild also represented a source of potential disruption. Wealth built on captive labor carried built-in instability.

That instability would matter when the Civil War came and split the Nation along many lines, one of them slavery.

Uneven Recovery

By the 1850s, observers described the Cherokee Nation in Indian Territory as relatively prosperous compared to many other Native communities pushed west. There were schools, churches, and newspapers. There were thriving farms and ranches, stores, mills, and salt works.

But this prosperity was uneven.

- A small group of slaveholding and commercially connected families held significant land, livestock, and capital.

- Many Cherokee households lived on smaller farms, with modest herds and little surplus.

- Enslaved Black people remained property in law and were still performing much of the hardest work.

If you walked through the Nation at that time, you might see:

- a large two-story frame or brick house surrounded by broad fields, with enslaved people working under an overseer

- a cluster of small cabins and gardens where non-slaveholding Cherokees grew enough for their families and a little extra

- camps and quarters where enslaved families lived in cramped, controlled conditions

On paper, the national balance sheet looked healthier than it had in the immediate aftermath of removal. On the ground, the old inequalities of the East had been planted in new soil.

The Reconstruction Ledger

If we look at forced reconstruction in Indian Territory through the same fourfold ledger, it reads like this.

Value created

- cleared and fenced land for farms and ranches

- public buildings in Tahlequah and other centers

- salt works, mills, ferries, and roads

- schools and churches built on that physical base

Much of this value was created by the combined labor of enslaved Black people, non-slaveholding Cherokees, and other workers.

Value recorded

- national building accounts and contracts

- farm and business records

- census accounts of improved land and livestock

Official documents mostly bore the names of Cherokee owners, contractors, and office holders.

Value captured

- slaveholding families recovered and grew wealth fastest, using enslaved labor to expand acreage, diversify businesses, and leverage credit

- the Nation as a government benefited from increased tax revenue and infrastructure, while allocating influence and contracts largely through the same elite networks

Value excluded or redirected

- enslaved Black people remained property in law, with no recognized claim to land or the value of their work

- non-slaveholding Cherokees rebuilt slower and faced more risk from crop failure or debt

- women lost formal political power even as their labor remained vital in households and farms

This reconstruction set the stage for everything that followed. When the Civil War came, it tore through a society already built on unequal shares of land, capital, and power. When emancipation arrived in law, it landed in a Nation whose physical and economic base had been built in large part by the people now called freedmen.

The next chapter turns to that moment. It looks at freedom, citizenship, and the cost of belonging for Black people in the Cherokee Nation after the Civil War and the Treaty of 1866.

CHAPTER 5

Freedom, Citizenship, and the Cost of Belonging

When the guns finally fell quiet in the 1860s, "freedom" did not arrive in the Cherokee Nation as a simple gift. It arrived as a bargain backed by treaties, arguments, and fear.

On paper, slavery ended in three strokes.

In 1863, the Cherokee National Council passed its own act abolishing slavery.
In 1865, the wider Civil War ground to a close.
In 1866, a new treaty with the United States confirmed emancipation and promised that former slaves of Cherokee citizens and certain free Black residents, and their descendants, "shall have all the rights of native Cherokees."

Those words look clean in a printed treaty. In real life, they landed on a society whose fields, buildings, and balance sheets still rested on the unpaid labor of Black people.

This chapter follows what happened next.

We look at how freedom was defined, how citizenship for Black people was written into law, how it was resisted and narrowed, and what it cost Black Cherokees and Cherokee Freedmen to try to claim what the treaty said they already had.

Emancipation in Cherokee Law

The Cherokee Nation did not wait for the 1866 treaty to put abolition into its own code.

In 1863, in the middle of the Civil War, a national act declared that "slavery and involuntary servitude, except for crime, are forever prohibited in this Nation." Historians of Cherokee law and the Civil War era point to that act as a turning point in national policy, though its enforcement on the ground was uneven.

The 1863 act did not by itself answer the big question that came next.

If enslaved Black people were no longer property, what were they in relation to the Nation.

Subjects.
Strangers living among citizens.
Citizens in their own right.

The Treaty of 1866 gave one answer. It made emancipation part of a bilateral agreement and tied it directly to citizenship. It committed the Nation to treat former slaves of Cherokee citizens and certain free Black residents, and their descendants, as citizens with the "rights of native Cherokees."

In theory, that settled the matter.

In practice, the treaty opened a new fight inside the Nation over who belonged to the "we," who counted for land and money, and how far white and federal pressure could reach into tribal sovereignty.

Who Was a Citizen

After the Civil War, Native nations that had sided with or been allied to the Confederacy, including the Cherokee Nation, were forced to negotiate new treaties with the United States. For Cherokee leaders, one of the hardest parts of the 1866 treaty was the clause on Black people.

The treaty language did three key things on status:

- It confirmed the end of slavery in Cherokee law.

- It recognized the former slaves of Cherokee citizens and certain free Blacks as citizens.

- It extended that citizenship to their descendants, with all the rights of native Cherokees.

That meant, in principle, that Black men and women who had been property a few years before were now:

- entitled to vote in Cherokee elections (if they met the same conditions as others)

- entitled to hold land in the Nation

- entitled to share in public benefits such as schools and annuities

This was not a minor adjustment in a corner of the law. It was a redefinition of the Nation's membership.

For Black people who had worked, suffered, and built in the Nation for decades, the new status was more than symbolic. It meant they could finally appear in the national ledger as persons with claims, not just as unlisted creators of value.

The backlash was immediate.

Some Cherokee citizens accepted the change as part of the new order. Others argued that the United States had forced the Nation to accept non-Cherokees as members and that this violated sovereignty. They claimed that Black people could live in the Cherokee Nation but should not be counted as full citizens.

Those debates played out in council sessions, local politics, and daily life for years.

Land, Labor, and the Cherokee Freedmen

For newly emancipated Black people in the Cherokee Nation, the most urgent question after 1866 was not abstract. It was simple.

Where can we live, and on what land.

Unlike in much of the former Confederacy, where US Freedmen were promised "forty acres and a mule" and then largely denied it, Cherokee Freedmen entered a Nation whose entire land base was still formally held in common by the Nation. There was no immediate system of individual allotments. Citizens could claim and improve tracts of public domain land, build houses and fields, and expect the Nation to recognize those improvements as theirs as long as they remained citizens.

Because the treaty recognized Cherokee Freedmen as citizens, they could do the same.

In practice, this meant that:

- Cherokee Freedmen families settled on open land in various districts.

- They built cabins, fenced fields, and planted crops.

- They founded churches and schools.

- They formed communities that would, over time, be known as Black Cherokee towns and neighborhoods.

These places were not gifts. They were built from the same mix of hard labor and fragile security that had defined Black life before emancipation. The difference was that, on paper, Cherokee law now treated these families as members of the Cherokee Nation, not as property of other members.

That legal status mattered when disputes arose.

A Cherokee Freedman who had improved a piece of land might stand before a Cherokee court and argue that no one could simply push him off. A widow might claim her right to remain on a farm after her husband's death. A congregation might seek recognition for its school as part of the public system.

Every one of those claims reached back to the 1866 treaty's language of equal rights, even if the people invoking it did not quote it word for word.

The Cost of Belonging

Citizenship did not erase racism.

In daily life, Black Cherokees and Cherokee Freedmen still faced discrimination and violence. Some Cherokees refused to accept them as social equals. Intermarriage between Black and Cherokee people could be stigmatized. Tensions over labor, wages, and status remained sharp.

At the same time, citizenship came with obligations.

Cherokee Freedmen citizens paid taxes in the ways the law required. They were subject to conscription and other duties when those applied to Cherokee men. They could be drawn into factional conflicts and suffer consequences when they picked a side.

The "cost of belonging" worked in at least three directions.

1. **Material cost**
    Cherokee Freedmen often had to prove membership again and again to secure land, schooling, and aid. That meant time, money for travel and petitions, and a constant fight against attempts to reclassify them as outsiders when money was at stake.

2. **Social cost**
    Black Cherokees risked rejection both from some Native neighbors who did not see them as "real" Cherokees and from outside Black communities who sometimes questioned ties to a Native Nation that had owned slaves. Navigating those lines took emotional labor and careful choices.

3. **Political cost**
    Claiming treaty rights put Cherokee Freedmen in direct conflict with powerful interests, including some leaders who

wanted to narrow the Cherokee Nation's membership to people they defined as "by blood."

Despite those costs, Cherokee Freedmen communities repeatedly chose to claim the Nation rather than walk away from it.

They enlisted in its future because their labor and ancestors had built its past.

Cherokee Freedmen in the Public Ledger

One way to see the new status of Cherokee Freedmen is to watch how they show up in public spending.

In the decades after 1866, the Cherokee Nation funded schools, including schools designated for Cherokee Freedmen children in certain districts. It hired teachers, bought supplies, and built or supported schoolhouses where Black Cherokee children could learn reading, writing, and arithmetic.

Those line items in the budget were not charity. They were, in theory, part of the Nation's obligation to all its citizens.

At the same time, public spending on Cherokee Freedmen services was often lower, more fragile, or more subject to challenge than spending on other schools. A single political shift could cut funds, close a building, or reduce salaries.

Beyond education, Cherokee Freedmen appear in payrolls and contracts. Black men worked as laborers on road crews, in mills, and on public works. Some held minor offices or local positions that came with small stipends. All of that represents value the Cherokee Nation paid out to Freedmen as citizens and in value Cherokee Freedmen gave back in labor and service.

Still, the larger picture did not change overnight.

The land itself remained communal, and the main tools for building wealth were:

- access to good land to improve

- access to credit and tools

- access to markets

On each of those fronts, Cherokee Freedmen often had less. They worked harder to reach the same level of security and were more vulnerable to shocks such as bad harvests, disease, or policy changes.

Internal Arguments, External Pressure

The struggle over Cherokee Freedmen citizenship took place both inside the Nation and at the boundary with the United States.

Inside, Cherokee politicians argued about:

- whether the treaty clause on Freedmen was binding forever

- whether Cherokee Freedmen descendants who had moved away should be treated as citizens on the same footing

- whether the Cherokee Nation could, as an act of sovereignty, re define its membership to exclude people it had previously accepted

Some leaders maintained that Cherokee people had the right to set their own citizenship rules, even if that meant narrowing membership in ways that contradicted the 1866 treaty. Others insisted that a promise made in a treaty, especially one that ended a war, could not be taken back without destroying trust and law.

From outside, federal officials watched these debates with mixed motives.

Sometimes the United States pointed to treaty obligations and pressed the Cherokee Nation to honor Cherokee Freedmen rights, especially when it suited federal political goals. At other times, federal agents showed little interest in enforcing Cherokee Freedmen claims, focusing instead on land and business matters that involved white settlers.

The result was a patchwork of partial enforcement, long lags, and legal ambiguities that would come back in the twentieth and twenty first centuries when Freedmen descendants again went to court.

Cherokee Freedom Without Security

By the late nineteenth century, it was clear that emancipation and citizenship had not erased the core problem that runs through this book.

Cherokee Freedmen and Black Cherokees still created value at high levels in agriculture, crafts, and small business. They were still under represented in the places where that value was recorded and where decisions were made. They still captured only part of what they built.

In the years just before allotment and Oklahoma statehood, Black Cherokees and Cherokee Freedmen descendants lived with a fragile kind of security. They had:

- land they had improved

- churches and schools they had built

- community networks they had woven

They also knew that:

- the United States was preparing to break up the communal land base

- white settlers were pressing in from all sides

- statehood would bring a new legal environment dominated by white laws and courts

The cost of belonging, in that context, was to stand in a Nation that still held their names in its laws but was increasingly pulled toward policies and alliances that could harm them.

The Ledger of Freedom

If we set the postwar and 1866 treaty era into the ledger frame, we can see why this chapter matters for the rest of the story.

Value created

- freed Black people continued to farm, clear land, raise families, and build institutions in the Nation

- their labor kept Cherokee agriculture and local economies alive after the war

Value recorded

- the Treaty of 1866 wrote Cherokee Freedmen citizenship into international law

- Cherokee statutes and rolls recorded some Cherokee Freedmen as citizens

- budgets and payrolls began to list Cherokee Freedmen schools and workers

Value captured

- some Cherokee Freedmen families secured land use, education for their children, and modest political influence

- Black Cherokees and Cherokee Freedmen began to build multi-generational communities on Cherokee soil as recognized members

Value denied or contested

- efforts inside the Nation to narrow or deny Cherokee Freedmen citizenship undercut treaty promises

- discrimination and unequal access to capital limited Black Cherokee wealth building

- external pressure from the United States pulled the Nation toward future policies, such as allotment, that would once again put Cherokee Freedmen and Black Cherokees at high risk

The promise of 1866 was real. It put Black Cherokees and Cherokee Freedmen on the books as citizens, not as property. The cost of making that promise real has stretched over more than a century and a half.

In the next chapter, we look at one specific piece of that cost and that promise. We trace how Black Cherokee education in the Nation, especially Cherokee Freedmen schools and teacher payrolls, functioned as a kind of public finance, turning tax revenue and treaty money into human capital that could not be as easily seized as land.

CHAPTER 6

Education as Public Finance: Freedmen Schools and Payrolls

When people talk about schools, they usually talk about lessons.

Reading.
Writing.
Arithmetic.

In the Cherokee Nation after the Civil War, schools were more than classrooms. They were small public treasuries. Every schoolhouse was a place where treaty money, tax revenue, and political decisions turned into salaries, books, and bricks. Every Cherokee Freedmen school was also a test of whether Black Cherokee citizens would be treated as part of the "we" who deserved those investments.

This chapter looks at education as infrastructure.

Not just as uplift.
Not just as charity.
As public finance.

We follow the money into school payrolls and budgets. We ask who got paid. We ask who did the teaching. We ask why Black Cherokee children in a one room schoolhouse matter just as much to the ledger as a big contract or a land lease.

School as a Public Contract

To run a school in the Cherokee Nation, you needed money and permission.

Land for the building.
Lumber and labor to raise it.

Someone to teach.

Someone to keep a list of who showed up.

After 1866, the Nation began to rebuild and expand its public school system in Indian Territory. There were schools for children on the "by blood" side of the roll, often closer to district centers and mission stations. There were also schools for Cherokee Freedmen communities, sometimes in smaller settlements, sometimes in the shadow of larger towns.

On paper, the difference between those schools shows up in a simple place.

Payroll.

The Nation hired teachers and sometimes support staff for schools that it recognized as part of its system. Those teachers received wages from public funds. They filed reports. They were part of a chain that ran from a log classroom to the national treasury.

When a Cherokee Freedmen school appeared on that list, it meant:

- Black Cherokee families had convinced the Nation to treat their children's education as a public duty, not a private favor

- money collected from all citizens, including Cherokee Freedmen, was coming back into Black communities in the form of salaries, books, and buildings

- Black Cherokee children were being treated, for that moment, as part of the future that the Nation was willing to invest in

The opposite was also true.

When a Cherokee Freedmen settlement had to scrape together funds on its own, pay a teacher out of church offerings or farm income, and beg for textbooks, it showed up in the ledger as a place where citizens were funding their own public good because the Cherokee Nation had not yet honored its full obligation.

Teachers on the Books

In a cash poor world, a school salary was not just a line item. It was survival.

Cherokee, Black, and sometimes white teachers in the Nation earned modest wages for work that demanded long days and high patience. They were paid in currency, sometimes in kind, often late, and always under the watch of officials who wanted reports and results.

For Freedmen schools, teacher pay had at least three layers of meaning.

1. **Income and status for the teacher**
   A teaching position was one of the very few ways a Black person in the Cherokee Nation could receive regular wages from the government. It placed the teacher in a strange position. Dependent on the Nation's goodwill. Yet also a respected figure in the local community, someone literate and trusted.

2. **Signal of public recognition**
   When the national treasurer signed off on a paycheck for a Cherokee Freedmen school teacher, it sent a signal. This settlement counts. These children count. Their minds are part of our future balance sheet.

3. **Channel for outside funds**
   In some periods, mission boards or federal programs supplemented local education funding. Where those streams flowed through Cherokee Freedmen schools, they brought extra books, training, or supplies. Wherever the Cherokee Nation allowed those funds in, it was making a choice about who would benefit.

Paying teachers, then, was not a neutral act. It was a small but real redistribution of public wealth. It could shrink the gap between communities. It could also widen it, if schools for some children were funded and staffed while others were left to fend for themselves.

Human Capital and the Long View

From the ledger angle, education looks different than land.

Land can be surveyed and sold.
Houses can be burned.
Livestock can be stolen.

But once a child learns to read, that cannot be taken with the same ease.

A child in a Cherokee Freedmen school who learned to read a deed, sign a contract, and follow a ledger, carried that skill for life. A girl who sat in a one room schoolhouse and practiced sums could grow into a woman who tracked prices, understood taxes, and held her own in the marketplace. A boy who read the newspaper aloud to elders could help his community see which laws were coming and which opportunities were real.

Economists call this "human capital." It is a cold term for a warm fact. Skills and knowledge increase a person's productive capacity and bargaining power.

For Black Cherokees and Cherokee Freedmen descendants, education had at least four economic effects:

- **Protection**
  Literate adults were harder to cheat. They could read contracts more easily and knew when a claim or tax was off.

- **Mobility**
  Education opened access to paid work beyond the field. Teaching, preaching, clerking, and small business all leaned on reading, writing, and arithmetic.

- **Institution building**
  Schools trained future church leaders, association officers, and community organizers. These people wrote minutes, petitions, and letters that moved money and policy.

- **Memory and record keeping**
  Educated community members could keep their own records

of land, births, deaths, and agreements. Those records could later be used in courts, allotment hearings, and claims.

In a world where Black land and Black wealth would come under attack again and again, investing in human capital was a way to store value in a place that was harder to seize.

Who Paid for Cherokee Freedmen Schools

Schools cost money from the first nail. The question in every community was "who pays."

In many Cherokee Freedmen settlements, the answer was "we do."

Black families pooled:

- church offerings

- crop money

- labor to cut logs and raise buildings

- clothing and food for teachers

Then they went to the Cherokee Nation and asked for help.

Sometimes they received:

- small stipends for teachers

- partial funding for repairs

- official recognition that allowed a school to be placed on the roll of public institutions

Sometimes they were denied or stalled.

Officials might argue that:

- the Nation could not afford more schools

- the population was too small to justify a separate Cherokee Freedmen school

- children could attend a school already operating for Cherokee citizens by blood

On the ground, those arguments often meant that Black children faced longer walks, colder welcomes, and a curriculum that did not reflect their lives.

When the Cherokee Nation chose to fund a Cherokee Freedmen school, it was not simply being generous. Cherokee Freedmen taxes and labor were already going into the general pot. Recognition meant that some of that value flowed back in a visible way.

When the Cherokee Nation chose not to fund, or to fund at a lower level, it sent another message.

You are citizens on paper.
You are extra when we plan the budget.

Education as a Political Bargain

Every appropriation is a vote.

When the council voted funds for the school system, it was choosing among priorities:

- buildings and repairs

- teacher salaries

- books and supplies

- special programs and new schools

Behind the numbers sat arguments about identity.

Should Cherokee Freedmen have separate schools, or should their children attend schools with other Cherokee children. Should Cherokee Freedmen communities have equal access to public

funds, or should their schools rely more heavily on missions and outside aid.
Should the curriculum for Cherokee Freedmen children include Cherokee language and history, or focus on English literacy and manual training.

Different factions answered those questions in different ways.

Some leaders, including Black Cherokees, argued that separate Freedmen schools risked creating a second tier inside the Cherokee Nation. Others believed that separate schools, if properly funded, gave Black children a safer and more affirming environment.

White missionaries had their own agendas, often mixing religious teaching with basic education and importing racial attitudes from outside.

Through it all, the underlying ledger question remained.

Who will control the flow of money into Black children's minds.

The Classroom Economy

Inside the schoolhouse, children lived the economic logic of their families every day.

A child might miss days during planting and harvest seasons because her labor was needed in the field. A teacher might stretch lessons with slates and chalk because there were no fresh books. Older students sometimes taught younger ones in exchange for small favors or simply because the teacher needed help.

Even the layout of the day reflected economic priorities:

- mornings for reading and spelling

- afternoons for arithmetic and writing

- occasional lessons in bookkeeping, sewing, or farm math

Teachers in Freedmen schools often used whatever examples were available. Corn in a crib. Chickens in a yard. Wages for a day's work. Prices at a nearby store.

In that way, the classroom became a place where Black children learned not only how to read words, but how to read the world.

They learned that someone had to pay for the roof over their heads.
They learned that salaries could be cut. They learned that a missing textbook might reflect a missing appropriation far away.

They also learned that, despite all of that, they could master skills that their grandparents and parents had been punished for seeking.

Undervalued Teachers, Overvalued Excuses

By all accounts, teachers in Freedmen schools were underpaid and overworked compared to many of their peers.

They ran:

- larger classes

- classrooms with fewer supplies

- longer terms of service in communities with high needs

When budgets were tight, their salaries were among the first to be delayed. When political winds shifted, Freedmen schools were among the first to be threatened.

Officials used familiar excuses:

- "There is not enough money for all"

- "We must prioritize the children of Cherokees by blood"

- "Mission boards can help Cherokee Freedmen more"

Underneath those excuses was a simple fact.

Every dollar not paid to a Cherokee Freedmen teacher was a dollar that could be spent elsewhere.

The ledger of public finance is always about choices. In this case, the choice to shortchange Black education helped keep gaps in human capital and political understanding in place, which in turn made it easier to push through land policies and identity rules that would harm Freedmen most.

Education as Quiet Resistance

Despite all the obstacles, Cherokee Freedmen schools and Black teachers in the Cherokee Nation built a quiet kind of resistance.

They turned:

- tax dollars and treaty funds into skills that would later be used in court challenges and organizing

- young readers into adults who could track allotment notices, oil leases, and lease payments

- shared classrooms into networks of kin and community that would reach into towns like Muskogee, Foreman, and eventually Greenwood

In later decades, when Black Cherokees and Cherokee Freedmen descendants argued cases in tribal and federal courts, or ran businesses, or organized for civil rights, they were drawing on the human capital created in these rooms.

The importance of that investment did not always show up in budgets. It showed up in who could stand at a podium, write a petition, or read a contract aloud for elders.

The School Ledger

If we chart Cherokee Freedmen schools as part of the Nation's ledger, the pattern looks like this.

Value created

- literacy, numeracy, and civic understanding among Black children

- teaching positions and local employment

- networks of educated adults who could serve as leaders, record keepers, and advocates

Value recorded

- school budgets and teacher payrolls

- official lists of schools, including some designated for Cherokee Freedmen

- reports on attendance and performance, filed with the national government

Value captured

- Black Cherokees and Cherokee Freedmen descendants gained skills that could not be as easily stolen as land

- some communities secured school buildings and consistent teaching that increased their internal strength

Value denied or restricted

- unequal funding and delayed pay for Cherokee Freedmen schools reduced the scale of the gains

- political resistance to full inclusion of Cherokee Freedmen in the public system kept some children in under resourced or unofficial schools

- mission dependence sometimes gave outside bodies more say over Black education than Black communities themselves

Cherokee Freedmen schools did not fix the whole imbalance. They did something important within it. They turned part of the Cherokee Nation's revenues, and part of the promise of the 1866 treaty, into a different kind of wealth that could be carried forward in minds rather than deeds.

In the next part of the book, we turn from schools to the broader flows of money in the Cherokee Nation. We look at communal revenue, per capita payments, and the rigorous sorting of who counted as a citizen when cash and land distributions were on the line.

CHAPTER 7

Who Gets Paid: Communal Wealth and Identity Filters

By the late nineteenth century, money began to arrive in the Cherokee Nation that did not come from corn, cattle, or local taxes. It came from leases, sales, and federal arrangements on communal land.

The biggest of these was the Cherokee Outlet.

On maps, the Outlet looks like a long strip of land stretching west from the main Cherokee Nation into what is now northern Oklahoma. On the books, it looks like a block of value that belonged to the Nation as a whole, not to any one family. When that block began to generate cash, a simple question turned explosive.

Who gets paid.

This chapter is about communal wealth and identity filters.

We look at how money from shared resources was supposed to reach citizens.
We watch how categories such as "by blood" and "Freedman" were used to open or close the gate.
We trace how the answer to "who gets paid" reshaped the meaning of Cherokee citizenship for Black Cherokees and their descendants.

The Outlet as a Common Asset

The Cherokee Outlet was more than a strip on a map. It was grazing land, lease land, and, in the eyes of Cherokee law, part of the common estate of the Nation.

In the second half of the nineteenth century, the Outlet became important for two reasons:

- white cattlemen wanted to graze herds there and were willing to pay

- the United States wanted the land itself opened to non-Indian settlement

At first, the Nation leased grazing rights to cattle companies. Those leases brought in significant revenue. Later, under pressure from the federal government, the Nation agreed to cede the Outlet for a fixed sum. The most cited figure for the final payment is a little over eight and a half million dollars, though there were disputes over how much was actually paid and how.

For the Cherokee Nation as a political body, the Outlet money represented:

- compensation for the loss of a large communal land base

- a chance to pay off debts

- a fund that could be used for schools, services, and per capita distributions

The key word is "communal."

By treaty and tradition, the land had belonged to the Cherokee Nation as a whole. When it was leased or sold, the money that came in did not belong only to a subset of citizens. It belonged, in principle, to everyone the Nation recognized as part of itself.

That is where things broke down.

From Land to Paper to Cash

The transformation of the Outlet from land to cash followed a familiar pattern.

First, the United States pressured the Nation to agree to cession. Second, negotiators haggled over acreage and price.

Third, Congress appropriated funds and set terms. Fourth, money began to move, often late and unevenly.

On the Cherokee side, the national government had to decide:

- how much of the Outlet money to use for general expenses

- how much to apply to specific projects

- whether, and how, to divide any of it in per capita payments to citizens

Per capita distribution meant cutting the communal pot into equal shares and sending those shares directly to individual citizens, usually as cash payments or credits.

The question of per capita payments quickly turned into a question about rolls.

To divide the money, the Cherokee Nation needed a list of people to pay. That list was supposed to include all citizens. By the late nineteenth century, with the Dawes Commission at work and federal pressure building for allotment, multiple rolls existed or were being prepared, including:

- rolls of Cherokees "by blood"

- rolls of Cherokee Freedmen

- special categories for adopted groups

Those rolls did not just sort people on paper. They sorted people at the pay window.

A Simple Question with Complicated Answers

In a just world, the question "who gets paid" would have had a simple answer.

Every Cherokee Nation citizen.

Cherokee Freedmen had been recognized as citizens by the 1866 treaty. Their descendants lived on Cherokee land, farmed, sent children to schools, and paid taxes. When communal land produced cash, they had a claim.

Many Cherokees understood it that way and argued for inclusive distributions.

Others did not.

As debates over Outlet funds and other revenue grew sharper, some leaders and factions advanced a narrower answer:

Only those listed as Cherokees "by blood" should share in per capita payments.

This position rested on a misreading and recasting of identity. It treated the "by blood" label, originally a way to categorize people on federal rolls, as if it were the only true marker of belonging. It treated Cherokee Freedmen citizens, whose status rested on treaty language and Cherokee law, as if they were permanent guests.

When money sat in the pot, that difference in view turned into conflict.

Identity as a Gate

To see how identity categories became filters, imagine the sequence at a payout.

Officials decide that a portion of Outlet money will be divided per capita. They determine the amount each eligible citizen will receive. They produce a list of names.

If that list includes both "Cherokee by blood" and Cherokee Freedmen roll citizens, then each citizen receives a share. The communal asset is translated into private cash in a way that honors the 1866 promise.

If that list includes only "by blood" citizens, then Cherokee Freedmen and their descendants are treated as if they do not belong, even if they are standing in the same line, living in the same Nation, and farming the same soil.

The act of handing out money becomes an act of defining the body politic.

On the books, that decision looks like a technical choice about eligibility. In homes, it feels like theft.

You worked the land.
Your ancestors cleared the Outlet and drove cattle.
The Cherokee Nation signs a deal and gets paid.
You watch others collect while you are told to stand aside.

The Per Capita Fight

Arguments over per capita distributions were never just about one payment. They were about what kind of Nation Cherokee leaders believed they ran.

Some council members and citizens argued:

- that per capita payments were dangerous because they drained communal assets

- that funds should stay in the treasury for schools, roads, and long-term projects

- that the Outlet money should be treated as a trust for future generations

Others, including many ordinary citizens, argued:

- that Outlet and lease money represented years of land use and opportunity costs already borne by the living

- that it was only fair to share some of the proceeds in direct payments

- that ordinary families needed cash to pay debts, buy tools, and stabilize their lives

Inside those positions sat the question of Freedmen eligibility.

Opponents of Cherokee Freedmen claims sometimes used more general arguments. They said that only "true Cherokees" should share in national wealth. By "true," they often meant people who could trace enrollment to older rolls that did not include Black people.

Supporters of Cherokee Freedmen rights pointed back to the treaty and to the years of work Black Cherokees had given to the Nation. They insisted that citizenship could not be split into first class and second-class levels when money was on the table.

In the end, the way specific distributions were handled varied over time. In some cases, Cherokee Freedmen did receive shares. In others, they were excluded or shorted. What matters for this book is not just the exact outcome in any given year, but the pattern of using identity to open and close the gate, especially as allotment approached.

Communal Wealth, Racialized Risk

Communal assets such as the Outlet and other shared resources had an unusual property.

They belonged to the whole Nation on paper, yet they were under constant threat from outside.

The federal government could:

- refuse to pay fair value

- delay payments

- attach conditions

- threaten further land loss if deals were not accepted

Inside the Cherokee Nation, leaders had to decide how to respond and how to spread the resulting risk.

If communal land was ceded at a discount, everyone lost something in principle. But in practice, the burden fell unevenly.

- Wealthy families who already owned good land in the core Nation, or who had businesses and livestock, had other sources of income and assets.

- Poorer citizens, including many Cherokee Freedmen, had fewer buffers. Cash from communal deals could mean the difference between hanging on and falling behind.

When identity filters denied Cherokee Freedmen full access to per capita payments or other benefits from communal assets, those families bore a double loss:

- they lost their share of a common inheritance

- they still bore the general harms of communal land shrinkage, such as crowding, reduced grazing, and growing pressure from outside

From the ledger angle, this was a form of value redirection.

Value created in part by Black Cherokee labor and shared Cherokee use of land was being turned into cash. That cash was being directed primarily to a subset of citizens defined by blood language, not by shared history.

Paper Citizenship, Real Exclusion

On paper, the status of Cherokee Freedmen remained anchored in the Treaty of 1866 and in subsequent laws that recognized them as citizens.

In lived experience, those rights were constantly tested at the point where paper met money.

When a Cherokee Freedman farmer went to claim a per capita payment and was told he was not on the right roll, he learned that the Cherokee Nation's promise had conditions. When a Cherokee Freedmen settlement saw "by blood" schools opened nearby while their own school struggled for funds, they saw how categories affected public spending. When roads or improvements were directed first to towns dominated by "by blood" citizens, they saw the same pattern again.

These were not isolated incidents. They formed a network of small exclusions that added up over time.

The ledger records them as:

- value created by Black and Native labor

- value recorded under the Cherokee Nation's name

- value captured by those inside the "by blood" gate

- value denied to those outside it, even when they were citizens in law

This everyday experience of being both inside and outside would shape how Cherokee Freedmen descendants understood later events such as allotment and statehood. When the time came to divide land itself into individual parcels, they already knew what it meant to be on the wrong side of the line.

Choosing Between Pot and People

There is another dimension to the Outlet story that reaches beyond identity labels. It is the tension between keeping money in the communal pot and letting people draw from it directly.

Leaders who opposed per capita distributions, or who wanted to limit them, sometimes made entirely rational arguments:

- communal funds could support schools, health care, and public buildings that benefited everyone

- large per capita payouts could encourage short term spending and leave nothing for long term needs

- in a world of constant federal pressure, keeping money in the treasury was a way to preserve some autonomy

Those arguments were not wrong in the abstract.

The problem came when they were used selectively.

If a government calls for sacrifice and long-term thinking from some citizens while quietly channeling other benefits to a favored group, the burden is not shared. People notice.

For Black Cherokees and Cherokee Freedmen descendants, calls to keep money in the communal pot often sounded hollow when they saw:

- school funding favors

- identity based exclusions from certain distributions

- contracts and opportunities going to the same families repeatedly

They lived in a world where they were asked to think as members of a national "we," but were treated as "they" when wealth moved.

The Outlet Ledger

We can track the Outlet story and similar communal wealth questions in the same four-way ledger.

Value created

- grazing, farming, and development on communal lands over decades

- negotiation capacity built by leaders, including Black and Native citizens, who understood markets and law

Value recorded

- lease contracts, cession agreements, and federal appropriations

- national budgets that logged Outlet and other communal revenue

Value captured

- the Cherokee Nation as a whole received large payments that could be used to pay debts and fund services

- per capita distributions, when inclusive, placed cash directly into households that had endured land loss and economic shocks

Value redirected or denied

- when the price for the Cherokee Outlet came in below its real value, the difference flowed to the United States and later to settlers who used the land

- when identity filters such as "by blood" excluded Cherokee Freedmen citizens from distributions, their share of communal value was redirected to others inside the Nation

- when communal funds were spent in ways that favored certain communities over others, gaps in infrastructure and opportunity widened

The Cherokee Outlet is not the only example of this pattern, but it is one of the clearest. It shows how a shared resource can be turned into cash and that cash can be used to redraw the lines of belonging.

In the next chapter, we look at the moment when communal land itself was broken into individual parcels under federal allotment policy. We follow how land became paper, how that paper became a new set of ledgers, and how Black Cherokees and Freedmen descendants tried to defend their claims in a system designed to make land easier to lose.

CHAPTER 8

Allotment: When Land Became Paper

Before allotment, a Cherokee family's claim to land was simple.

You lived on it.
You cleared it.
You built a house, a smokehouse, a garden, a barn.
Your neighbors knew it was yours, and the Nation recognized your improvements on communal soil.

There were no individual deeds from a county courthouse. There were no tract numbers on a plat map.

Then, in the early 1900s, the United States brought in a different system. Surveyors, commissioners, and clerks turned the land of the Cherokee Nation into lines on paper and then assigned numbered parcels to named individuals. Under the Agreement with the Cherokee in 1902, each enrolled citizen was supposed to receive land equal in value to 110 acres of the average allotable land, with a separate homestead portion equal in value to forty acres.

The land did not move.
The ownership model did.

This chapter follows that shift.

We watch how land that had been held in common became personal property on paper. We look at how that paper carried different rules for different people. We see how Black Cherokees and Cherokee Freedmen entered an allotment system already wired with racial and legal risk.

From Nation Land to Individual Parcels

Allotment in the Cherokee Nation did not come directly from the first Dawes Act of 1887. That act targeted many tribes, but the Five Tribes, including the Cherokees, had separate treaties and had to be brought under individual allotment through specific agreements.

For the Cherokees, that agreement was approved in 1902. It said, in plain treaty prose:

- each citizen of the Cherokee tribe, once enrolled, would receive land equal in value to 110 acres of average land

- the allotment should include the citizen's existing improvements as far as possible

- out of that allotment, the citizen would select a homestead equal in value to forty acres, with a separate certificate and special protection from sale for a set period

The Dawes Commission, working under this and similar agreements, used new rolls and surveys to turn citizens into individual allottees and to turn communal land into numbered tracts.

On the ground, this meant survey stakes and strangers.

A family that had lived on a piece of land for decades watched government men measure and mark it. They were told which part they could claim as a homestead. They were told what their "surplus" acres were worth. Those acres might not even be continuous. In some cases, people found that part of their allotment was far from home, in an area they had never seen.

For Black Cherokees and Cherokee Freedmen, the process was the same on paper. The Dawes' categories were, Citizens by blood, Freedmen, Intermarried White, and Adopted. So, Cherokee Freedmen were on separate categories of the Dawes rolls but were recognized as Cherokee citizens. Studies of Oklahoma Indian titles note that about 40,196 Cherokees, including roughly 4,924 Cherokee Freedmen, received average allotments of 110 acres, with a forty-acre homestead portion.

The roll category you were placed on, however, would matter later.

Land as a Bundle of Rules

Allotment did not give every Cherokee citizen the same kind of title.

The Agreement with the Cherokee required:

- a homestead portion, equal in value to about forty acres, that was inalienable during the allottee's lifetime, up to twenty-one years

- a separate certificate for the homestead

- restrictions for a period on selling or encumbering the rest of the allotment

Congress then layered additional statutes on top of those treaty terms, including the Act of April 26, 1906 and the Act of May 27, 1908, which tightened or relaxed restrictions based on blood quantum and status.

By 1908, one rule in particular shaped the future:

- restrictions on alienation were removed from the allotments of members of the Five Tribes with less than one half Indian blood, intermarried white citizens, and Freedmen

- full blood citizens kept restrictions for a longer period, often twenty-five years, unless Congress lifted them earlier

In everyday terms, that meant:

- many "by blood" Cherokees, especially those recorded as full blood, had land that was legally harder to sell or lose quickly

- many Freedmen allottees had land that became fully taxable and sellable much sooner

The federal government framed these restrictions as protection. Supreme Court opinions described them as part of the United States' ongoing guardianship over Indian wards.

Protection can be a two-sided word.

If your land is heavily restricted, it is harder to lose, but you may struggle to use it as collateral. If your land is unrestricted, you have more formal freedom, but you are exposed to taxes, debt, fraud, and hard sales pressure.

For many Black Cherokees and Freedmen, allotment assigned them to the second category.

The Dawes Rolls as Destiny

The Dawes Rolls were enrollment lists, not land records, but they became the base layer for allotment and later for restrictions. They split people into categories such as:

- Cherokee by blood

- Cherokee by intermarriage

- Cherokee Freedmen

Applications and records for allotment were then organized by tribe and designation.

Those labels were not simple reflections of identity. They were a mix of genealogy, appearance, testimony, and politics.

For Black Cherokees with Black and Cherokee ancestry, the category "Freedman" often erased the "by blood" reality of their Cherokee line and tied their legal future to the 1866 treaty clause on former slaves instead of to the older kinship and clan systems of the Cherokee Nation.

When Congress tied restrictions on land to blood quantum and used the Dawes Rolls to measure that quantum, these labels hardened into tools:

- "By blood" rolls became the reference point for who would keep restricted land longer

- "Freedmen" rolls became associated with land that federal law treated more like non-Indian property, taxable and freely alienable

- allotment records and later statutes used those categories again when setting up guardianships and testing "competency"

In other words, who you were on paper started to control how vulnerable your land was, even if your day-to-day life and ancestry were more complex than the roll lines admitted.

Guardianship and "Incompetence"

Once Cherokee land was broken into individual parcels, outside courts and federal officials developed new ways to separate Native and Black landowners from their holdings.

One tool was the legal label "incompetent."

Under federal and Oklahoma law in the early twentieth century, many Native allottees, especially full blood citizens, were presumed "incompetent" to manage the sale or lease of their land. Legal title often remained in trust, and county courts worked with federal agencies to approve or deny transactions.

In theory, this was protection. In practice, corruption and racism shaped who was declared incompetent and how guardians used their power.

Studies of allotment in Oklahoma describe a "panoply of corrupt county judges" who quickly declared Native landowners incompetent, appointed white guardians, and then approved sales of land that benefitted speculators far more than families.

Black allottees, including Native Freedmen and Black children like Sarah Rector in neighboring tribes, were also swept into guardianship systems. Courts decided they could not handle the money that flowed from land, especially if that land held oil or other resources. White guardians then controlled leases, royalties, and sales.

This did not look like the old slave market, but the logic had a familiar edge:

- declare a person legally unequal

- appoint someone from the dominant group to "protect" them

- move the asset while calling the process lawful

For Native Freedmen whose land was already less protected by restriction, the guardianship system turned "freedom" into another point of exposure.

You   were   no   longer   property. Your land was still treated as something you were not fully trusted to manage.

Taxes, Titles, and Forced Sales

As restrictions lifted and Oklahoma became a state in 1907, another kind of pressure arrived. Taxes.

Under the 1908 act and related statutes, land from which federal restrictions had been removed was subject to state and local taxation. Courts held that when restrictions were gone, allotted lands could be taxed and, if taxes were not paid, sold at auction.

For many Cherokee Freedmen families, that meant:

- land that had been tax free under tribal communal ownership suddenly carried annual bills

- any gap in cash flow, such as a bad crop year or illness, could lead to unpaid taxes

- unpaid taxes could lead to county sales, with land passing into white ownership for pennies on the dollar

Title attorneys and later scholars have traced how allotment, restriction policy, tax sales, and county court decisions produced a massive transfer of land out of Native and Black hands in eastern Oklahoma.

The pattern was not random.

- land with high resource value, such as oil or town sites, drew the most aggressive legal attention

- guardianship cases focused on people with promising allotments

- tax sales often centered on tracts whose owners lacked cash and legal help

Native Freedmen lands, often unrestricted and taxable early, sat right at the intersection of these pressures.

Paper Mistakes, Real Losses

Another quiet channel of land loss was simple paperwork.

Allotment required:

- correct names on Dawes Rolls

- clear descriptions of tracts

- accurate recording of deaths and heirs

Any error could cause trouble:

- if a name was spelled differently across documents, someone could claim a sale or lease was valid when it was not

- if an heir was left off a list, their share might be absorbed by others or sold without their knowledge

- if a land description used the wrong section or range, disputes over boundaries could drag on for years

For well connected families with lawyers and political clout, such errors could sometimes be fixed. For poor families, including many Black Cherokees and Cherokee Freedmen, a bad document could mean the effective end of their claim.

The National Archives still holds "allotment jackets," files for individual allottees that include maps, correspondence, and legal paperwork. Looking at a Native Freedman's jacket today, you might see:

- an original certificate of allotment

- a homestead designation

- later leases and deeds

- a guardian appointment

- tax notices or court orders

Each page is a record of how land moved or stayed. Many of those packets show land slipping away through a series of signatures and stamps rather than a single dramatic seizure.

Allotment for Those Already on the Margin

From a distance, allotment looks like a policy that treated all tribal citizens equally: 110 acres each in the Cherokee Nation, with a forty-acre homestead. Up close, the experience of allotment diverged sharply based on race, roll status, and access to support.

For many "by blood" Cherokees:

- restrictions kept land off the tax rolls for longer

- community networks sometimes helped protect homesteads

- some parcels were lost, but others remained in families into the present

For many Cherokee Freedmen and Black Cherokees:

- allotments were categorized in ways that made them unrestricted and taxable sooner

- county courts and guardianship systems treated them as targets for management and sale

- they faced discrimination in access to credit and legal aid, making it harder to hold on through hard years

In both groups, there were people who lost everything and people who maintained some holdings. The key point for the ledger is not to claim a single outcome, but to map the tilt.

The structure of allotment, blood-based restrictions, guardianship, and taxation placed Black Cherokees and Freedmen closer to the edge of loss from the start.

Their labor and that of their parents and grandparents had helped create the communal land base. Allotment converted that communal legacy into personal parcels under unequal rules.

The Allotment Ledger

If we lay allotment in the Cherokee Nation into the same four column ledger, it reads this way.

Value created

- survey and legal systems that clarified parcels for later use

- individual homesteads that some families held and improved over generations

- short term cash from leases and sales, sometimes used to buy tools, livestock, or education

Value recorded

- Dawes Rolls categorizing citizens as "by blood," "intermarried," "Freedmen," or "adopted"

- allotment certificates and patents setting out 110 acres in value, with a forty-acre homestead designation

- federal and state statutes defining restrictions, taxation, and guardianship

Value captured

- some Cherokee families, both "by blood" and Freedmen, used allotments to anchor long term land-based wealth

- the United States and white settlers gained clear, alienable title to "surplus" lands and to many parcels lost through guardianship, fraud, and tax sales

Value redirected or destroyed

- communal land that had sheltered all citizens became a checkerboard of private titles

- Black Cherokees and Cherokee Freedmen, whose lands were often less protected, lost a disproportionate share through early taxation and predatory legal processes

- the Nation's ability to use land policy as a collective tool weakened as more acres slipped into non-Cherokee ownership

Allotment turned land into paper and then let that paper decide who would still be standing in the next generation.

In the next part of the book, we narrow the focus. We leave the big treaties and statutes behind for a moment and look at how Black Cherokees and Cherokee Freedmen built everyday economies inside this legal storm: farms, ranches, shops, and networks of work that linked Indian Territory to places like Muskogee, Okmulgee, and eventually Greenwood.

CHAPTER 9

Labor That Built Value

Stand anywhere in late nineteenth century Indian Territory and listen.

You will hear a few loud voices.
Lawyers in court.
Traders arguing over prices.
Council members speaking in the square.

If you listen closer, you will hear something else.

Hooves in a corral at dawn.
Hoes cutting into dry ground.
Hammers on new boards.
Voices in a cotton row.

This quieter sound is what this chapter is about.

The labor of Black Cherokees and Cherokee Freedmen that turned treaty language and allotment maps into real value. Work that made the difference between a bare allotment and a working farm, between a patch of prairie and a town street. Work that rarely showed up in official stories, even when it sat right in the center of the scene.

From Bound Work to Paid Work

Emancipation ended slavery in law, but it did not end the need to work the land.

In the years after the Civil War and the Treaty of 1866, Cherokees Freedmen shifted from bondage to a mix of:

- small landholding and farming on their own account

- tenant farming and sharecropping arrangements

- wage labor on Cherokee and white farms

- paid work in construction, freight, and domestic service

The crucial difference was that, as citizens, Cherokee Freedmen could hold and improve land within the Nation. Many did just that. They settled on tracts in various districts, built cabins, fenced fields, and raised crops. Their farms often sat alongside those of Cherokees by blood, connected by kinship, marriage, and shared work as much as by roads.

At the same time, the old pattern did not vanish.

Planters and big stockmen still needed labor. Cherokee Freedmen who did not yet have land, or whose allotments had not been finalized, hired out by the season or year. Women continued to do domestic and care work in Cherokee households. Young men and boys took jobs herding cattle, driving wagons, and working in mills.

The form of the contract changed. The core reality did not.

Black people continued to create a large share of the Nation's agricultural and commercial value. Whether they captured that value for themselves depended on what kind of work they could secure and what kind of title they held underneath it.

Farms on the Edge

Walk into a Cherokee Freedmen farmyard in the 1880s or 1890s.

The house is modest.
The fields are smaller than some of the big ranch spreads.
The family is up before sunrise.

Corn and fodder crops fill most of the space. There might be a small cotton patch, or a few rows of another cash crop, if the family can risk the time and soil. Chickens scratch in the yard. A hog or two stands in a pen. A milk cow grazes close by.

This is not plantation agriculture. It is survival agriculture with ambition.

Every cleared acre and every fence line represents hundreds of hours of labor by men, women, and children. They cut and hauled timber, dug post holes, and pulled stumps. They planted, hoed, and harvested. They repaired tools that broke in hard ground.

On paper, that household might appear in a census as:

- a Cherokee Freedman head of household

- a wife

- several children

- a note about acreage and crops

In reality, it is a small economic unit doing at least three things:

- feeding itself

- producing a little surplus to sell in town

- trying to hold land against drought, debt, and the coming storm of allotment

When we talk later about Greenwood and Black entrepreneurship, it is important to remember that many of the people who moved into towns and cities started here, on small farms like this one, learning how to balance risk and work on land that could be taken or taxed away.

Hired Hands and Day Wages

Not every Black Cherokee or Cherokee Freedman had land or wanted to farm full time. Many moved through a patchwork of jobs.

Common kinds of work included:

- day labor on construction sites for houses, barns, and public buildings

- seasonal work on large farms and ranches, especially at planting and harvest

- chopping wood, hauling water, and maintaining fences for wages

- freight work, driving wagons between towns and depots

- domestic service in Cherokee and white households

Wages were low and often paid in a mix of cash and goods. A man might work from sunup to sundown and receive:

- a small coin payment

- meals

- credit at a local store

A woman working as a cook or laundress might be paid monthly, with deductions for food or lodging.

From the ledger angle, this kind of labor created value in a direct way:

- the employer could plant more acres, build more structures, or move more goods

- the wages kept the worker's family alive and occasionally allowed for small savings

The gap between the value created and the wages paid represented profit. The size of that gap depended on how tight the labor market was and how much bargaining power workers had.

For Black laborers, racism and limited opportunities kept wages low and bargaining power weak. The ledger entries for their work, when they appear at all, usually show up as expenses in someone else's account book, not as building blocks of their own net worth.

Women's Work, Uncounted and Central

Black Cherokee and Cherokee Freedmen women carried a double load in this era.

On farms, they:

- planted, weeded, and harvested

- tended gardens, chickens, and small livestock

- cooked, cleaned, and raised children

In towns and near wealthy households, they also:

- cooked for wages

- washed and ironed clothes

- sewed and mended

- took in boarders

Most of this labor never appears in official records. Census takers might mark a woman as "keeping house" without any note of the work she did beyond the walls. Pay records, when they exist, list her by first name next to a small sum.

Yet without this labor:

- men working day jobs would have lacked food and clean clothing

- children could not have gone to school

- churches and mutual aid societies would have lacked the quiet backbone that kept them running

From the economic side, women's labor turned:

- raw food into meals

- cloth into wearable clothing

- sick bodies into healed workers

It also produced small amounts of cash and credit that women sometimes controlled directly. In some Black Cherokee families, women kept the household accounts, tracked debts, and made decisions about when to take in extra work or when to refuse it.

When the book later turns to entrepreneurs and case studies, some of the men whose names appear as "owners" were standing on foundations built by this largely unrecorded work.

Skilled Hands and Crafts

Agricultural and domestic work were central, but they were not the whole story.

Many Black Cherokees and Cherokee Freedmen also worked in skilled and semi-skilled trades:

- blacksmithing

- carpentry and joinery

- wagon building and repair

- masonry and brickmaking

- mill operation

These skills often crossed the line between plantation and free settings. Enslaved craftsmen in the East had learned trades under compulsion. After emancipation, some of them used the same skills on their own account or for wages.

In Indian Territory, a Black carpenter could build houses for Cherokee and Black families alike. A Blacksmith could repair tools and shoe horses for anyone who had the money. A mill worker who understood gears and water flow could keep a community's grain moving.

Skilled workers sometimes earned higher wages than field hands, and they had more independence in choosing jobs. In a few cases, they parlayed that position into small businesses, hiring younger men as helpers and apprentices.

Even when they did not become business owners, these craftsmen were central to the physical infrastructure of Black Cherokee towns and neighborhoods. Churches, schoolhouses, and lodge halls all depended on them.

Work on the Roads and Rails

As the nineteenth century turned toward the twentieth, transportation networks in and around the Cherokee Nation expanded.

Roads improved, and railroads began to cut across the landscape, linking Indian Territory to regional markets. Towns such as Muskogee, Vinita, and Fort Gibson grew as rail and river hubs.

Black Cherokees and Cherokee Freedmen worked in this expansion in several ways:

- as road crews, grading and maintaining routes

- as teamsters, driving freight wagons between depots and smaller towns

- as section hands and laborers on rail lines, laying track and maintaining rights of way

- as porters and service workers in stations and nearby hotels

These jobs did not always pay better than farm work, but they offered:

- travel and exposure to wider markets

- access to information about prices, opportunities, and legal changes

- chances to carry news and ideas between Black communities

A Black teamster hauling goods between a Cherokee town and a railhead was not just moving cargo. He was a human conduit for stories, strategies, and warnings.

In later chapters, when we talk about how information moved into places like Greenwood, it is worth remembering that some of it traveled in the heads of people who had been on these roads for years.

Church, Lodge, and Mutual Aid

Not all economic labor was waged. Some of the most important work Black Cherokees and Cherokee Freedmen did was in voluntary organizations that sat between the household and the market.

Churches.
Lodges.
Benefit societies.

In these spaces, people:

- pooled small sums to help members during sickness, funerals, or crop failure

- organized building projects for meeting houses and schools

- trained deacons, teachers, and officers in reading, writing, and public speaking

The labor that built and maintained these institutions was unpaid or low paid, but it created real economic value:

- mutual aid reduced the shock of sudden expenses

- organized fundraising built capital assets such as buildings and land

- leadership training prepared people for later roles in business and politics

From a ledger standpoint, you could think of this as community capital. It lived in relationships and trust as much as in dollars, but it helped Black Cherokees and Cherokee Freedmen survive in a hostile environment.

When a Black farmer lost a crop, the church might organize a collection. When a widow struggled to hold onto an allotment after her husband's death, lodge brothers might help with legal fees or fieldwork.

These acts of care did not change federal law. They changed who made it through the next winter.

The Gap Between Work and Wealth

Across all these forms of labor, a pattern holds.

Black Cherokees and Cherokee Freedmen:

- worked more hours than many of their neighbors

- took on some of the hardest physical and emotional tasks

- created value at every level of the local economy

Yet they did not, as a group, accumulate wealth at the same rate as many Cherokees by blood or white settlers in the region.

The reasons were not personal failings. They were structural:

- unequal access to good land and secure title

- discrimination in wages and hiring

- violence and intimidation when Black success became too visible

- legal systems that made Black and Native land easier to strip through guardianship and tax sales

From the ledger angle, it looks like this:

- value created by Black labor shows up in crop totals, building records, and business accounts

- value recorded tends to appear under the names of employers, landowners, and officials

- value captured flows to those same parties, with only a portion flowing back in wages and smallholdings

- value denied or redirected appears in the form of lost land, blocked promotions, and unacknowledged contributions

Later chapters will show how some Black Cherokees and Cherokee Freedmen beat the odds and built substantial wealth anyway, particularly in ranching and towns. Those stories do not erase this broader pattern. They stand out against it.

Seeds of Greenwood

By the end of the nineteenth century, the labor of Black Cherokees and Cherokee Freedmen had done several things at once:

- rebuilt the Cherokee Nation's physical base after removal

- created and stabilized Black farming communities across Indian Territory

- trained a generation of men and women in the disciplines of hard work, saving, and cooperation

- built churches, lodges, and schools that connected people across districts

As railroads grew and towns expanded, some of the children of these communities began to seek opportunity in denser places: Muskogee, Okmulgee, Tulsa, and smaller Black towns.

The skills they carried:

- farm math and risk sense

- carpentry, blacksmithing, and other trades

- literacy and public speaking from schools and churches

would soon be applied in a new context.

In Greenwood, the Black district of Tulsa, these skills would build something that looked, for a moment, like a concentrated answer to centuries of exclusion.

Before we get to that, the next chapter looks at the quieter side of Black Cherokee wealth creation: the small businesses, shops, services, and professions that emerged inside and alongside the Cherokee Nation, built by people who had turned years of hard labor into a little capital and a lot of grit.

CHAPTER 10

Entrepreneurs of the Cherokee Nation

In the records, Black Cherokees and Cherokee Freedmen show up first as labor.

Farm hands.
Herdsmen.
Washwomen.
Wagon drivers.

If you look a little longer, another pattern appears.

Some of those same people begin to show up as "owner," "proprietor," "contractor," "teacher," "merchant." They move from the wage column into the receipts column. They are still working every hour of daylight, but now they have a sign on the door, a herd branded in their name, or a line of customers who know that their money is staying in Black hands.

This chapter follows that shift.

It looks at Black Cherokee and Cherokee Freedmen entrepreneurs who built farms, ranches, shops, and professional practices inside a legal world that did not plan for them to succeed. It does not pretend they were many. It does insist they mattered.

Why Business Mattered

For Black Cherokees and Cherokee Freedmen, business ownership was not a luxury. It was a defense.

Wage work could be cut. Day labor could vanish with one bad season. Even small farms needed cash for taxes, tools, and emergencies.

A steady business, even a modest one, meant:

- a flow of money that did not depend on one white employer

- a place where Black people could expect service and respect

- a platform to pay taxes on time and fight off county sales or predatory loans

The 1866 treaty had made former slaves of Cherokee citizens into citizens themselves, with rights to claim land and improve any open tract in the Nation. That access to land set Black Cherokees apart from many US Freedmen in the southern states, where access to property was sharply constrained. Economic research on the Cherokee Freedmen shows that this window helped raise Black home and farm ownership in the Cherokee Nation above comparable levels in the Deep South, at least for a time.

Entrepreneurship was the next step. Land gave a platform. A herd, a shop, or a service turned that platform into income.

Herds, Railbeds, and Contracts

The clearest example of a Black Cherokee entrepreneur using land and law to build a fortune is Zachariah "Zack" Foreman Sr., whose story gets a full chapter next. Here, he stands as a headline and a pattern.

Born enslaved in the Cherokee Nation in the 1840s and freed after the Civil War, Foreman used his status as a Cherokee citizen to claim land, raise cattle, and then do something unusual. In the 1890s he struck a deal with the Kansas City Southern Railroad. If he prepared the roadbed across his land, the company would lay the steel. With that agreement, his herd and his land became the base for a private rail spur that linked his operation directly to wider markets.

By the turn of the century, researchers describe him as one of the wealthiest Black men in Indian Territory, exceptional in a region where most former slaves, struggled to acquire even a little property.

Foreman's story is not just about genius or luck. It rests on several structural facts this book has already traced:

- access to free or low-cost land inside the communal Cherokee estate

- the ability, as a Cherokee Freedman citizen, to improve that land and hold it

- the presence of rail companies hungry for right of way across Indian Territory

- a willingness to read the world like a ledger and treat his labor and stock as capital, not just survival

Most Black entrepreneurs never had a personal rail line. Many did find smaller ways to use the same logic:

- running wagon services that connected farms to depots

- breeding better livestock and selling breeding services

- contracting to build fences, roads, or bridges for pay

In each case, they took skills learned in bondage or wage work and turned them into contracts that bore their own names.

Small Stores and Second Streets

Not all business was out on the range. In towns that sat inside or on the edge of the Cherokee Nation, Black entrepreneurs, including Cherokee Freedmen and other Black residents, began to carve out commercial space of their own.

By the late nineteenth and early twentieth centuries, places like Muskogee, Fort Gibson, and nearby towns in Indian Territory had Black business districts where:

- undertakers

- barbers

- grocers

- livery stable owners

- boarding house keepers

- restaurant operators

served Black customers who were often unwelcome or poorly treated elsewhere.

A historical survey of African American life in Muskogee remembers men like William Ragsdale, who opened an undertaking business in 1889. Working out of a converted livery stable, he provided funeral services to Black families at a time when white firms either refused their business or offered it on humiliating terms.

The same study lists Black physicians, builders, and other professionals operating in the city by the early 1900s. Their clients included both town residents and people from surrounding rural districts, among them Cherokee Freedmen who came in for supplies, medical care, or legal advice.

These businesses did several quiet things at once:

- They kept a portion of Black spending circulating in Black hands before it left town.

- They created jobs for younger people as clerks, apprentices, and helpers.

- They gave Black Cherokees and Freedmen places to meet, share news, and plan.

Even when the owner was not formally enrolled as a Cherokee citizen, the store itself sat on land that had once been part of the Cherokee communal estate and now formed part of the emerging economy of eastern Oklahoma.

Professional Paths: Teachers, Preachers, and Practitioners

Some Black Cherokees and Cherokee Freedmen turned education and public service into professional careers that had an entrepreneurial edge.

Teachers in Cherokee Freedmen schools, described earlier, were technically public employees. In practice, they worked like small business operators:

- raising part of their own support through board and local collections

- managing school supplies and repairs

- sometimes running side ventures such as tutoring, copying, or correspondence services

Preachers and church leaders also moved in this space. A pastor who held a steady pulpit could:

- organize building funds to construct larger sanctuaries

- sponsor mutual aid societies that acted like informal insurance

- invite lecturers and traveling professionals who brought in information and contacts

In some Black Cherokee communities, church officers helped members navigate allotment law, interpret tax notices, or connect with lawyers. That advisory role had economic weight.

A smaller number of Black professionals trained in medicine, dentistry, or law set up practices in towns. City directories from places like Muskogee list Black doctors, a dentist, bankers, and notaries in the early twentieth century.

For Black Cherokees and Cherokee Freedmen, seeing a Black physician or lawyer behind a desk was more than a symbol. It meant:

- legal and medical advice from someone who understood tribal rolls, allotment, and local prejudice

- one more point where money spent might return to Black communities as wages, property, and philanthropy

These professionals often walked a careful line. They needed white and Native clients to survive financially, but they also faced resentment when their success became visible.

Business in Three Legal Worlds

Every Black Cherokee business operated inside a tangle of law.

1. **Tribal law** from the Cherokee Nation, with its rules on citizenship, land, and taxes.

2. **Federal law**, including treaties, allotment rules, and guardianship statutes.

3. **Territorial, then state law**, once Oklahoma began to move toward statehood and segregation.

A Freedman stockman might:

- rely on Cherokee citizenship to claim land and graze cattle

- sign federal allotment papers that turned part of that land into a personal title

- face county judges and state tax collectors once restrictions lifted

Economic research on this period shows that Cherokee Freedmen as a group were more likely to own farms and homes than Black people in the former Confederate states, largely because they could claim land after 1866 instead of relying on sharecropping. At the same time, the removal of federal restrictions from many Freedmen allotments left them exposed to taxes and forced sales earlier than some "by blood" neighbors.

Entrepreneurs had to read this landscape like a contract:

- using tribal status where it helped

- watching for federal moves that might change restrictions

- navigating new Oklahoma laws that enforced segregation in public life

A mistake could cost a herd, a storefront, or a homestead. A good judgment, like Foreman's rail deal, could shift a family's fortunes for a generation.

Circulating the Black Cherokee Dollar

Inside Black Cherokee communities, people knew instinctively that who owned a business mattered.

A dollar spent at a Black owned store might:

- pay the clerk

- pay the owner's taxes

- keep a Black family on their allotment

- fund a scholarship or a church roof

The same dollar spent at a white owned store might leave the community entirely.

This is not romantic. It is ledger work.

In many settlements, the circulation looked something like this:

1. A Cherokee Freedman farmer sells corn or livestock, often at a discounted price.

2. He uses that cash to buy necessities at a local Black owned store, or pays a Black smith to repair tools.

3. The store owner or smith then pays church dues, lodge fees, and property taxes, and sometimes hires help.

4. The church and lodge use those funds to support widows, cover doctor bills, or send a promising young person to school.

Each step keeps more of the value created by Black labor inside the community before it leaks into the wider market. In a hostile environment, that extra turn or two of the dollars can make the difference between hanging on and slipping under.

Risk, Hostility, and the Ceiling

None of this happened in a vacuum. Black success in business often drew hostile attention.

As Oklahoma moved from territory to statehood in 1907, lawmakers put segregation into state law. Public facilities, transportation, and schools were formally split by race. In daily practice, Black entrepreneurs faced:

- white competition backed by easier access to capital and credit

- racism from suppliers and officials who could refuse licenses or favorable terms

- threats and violence, especially when business districts flourished visibly

Some Black business districts sat in literal low ground, on flood prone or less desirable land, because white businesses had already claimed the prime locations. Others were squeezed by zoning and selective enforcement of codes.

Cherokee politics also shaped the ceiling. As identity debates hardened around "by blood" language, some Black Cherokees found it harder to claim tribal contracts or assistance, despite their legal citizenship. When communal funds were used for business development or public works, they did not always flow to Cherokee Freedmen neighborhoods at the same rate.

Black Cherokee entrepreneurs learned to diversify their defenses:

- spreading investments across land, livestock, and inventory

- building relationships with sympathetic officials and neighbors

- keeping their books in order to fight legal challenges

Even then, the ceiling was real. The average Cherokee Freedmen farmer or shopkeeper never achieved the wealth of a Foreman. Many saw their gains wiped out by allotment related losses, tax sales, or the general downturns that hit rural Oklahoma.

The Entrepreneurial Ledger

If we run Black Cherokee entrepreneurship through the same four-part ledger as earlier chapters, the pattern is clear.

Value created

- herds, crops, and freight contracts that linked Indian Territory to regional markets

- stores, services, and professional practices that met Black community needs

- churches, lodges, and schools financed in part by Black owned business income

Value recorded

- business licenses, contracts, and tax rolls that listed Black Cherokees and Cherokee Freedmen as proprietors

- articles and advertisements in local papers that named Black undertakers, doctors, merchants, and ranchers

Value captured

- some families converted labor and land access into lasting assets: cattle, town lots, savings, and, in rare cases, major enterprises like private rail spurs

- Black communities gained a measure of local control over services, prices, and space

Value denied or stripped

- unequal access to credit, discriminatory law, and racially skewed land restrictions limited how far most Black entrepreneurs could climb

- county courts, guardianship systems, and tax sales transferred many Black owned parcels and businesses into white hands over time

Even with those limits, Black Cherokee entrepreneurs did something lasting. They proved, in ledgers and not just in speeches, that Black people in the Cherokee Nation could own, manage, and grow capital in the middle of a system that often treated them as expendable.

In the next chapter, we slow down and focus on one of them in detail. We look closely at Zachariah "Zack" Foreman Sr., his cattle, his railroad, and the way his wealth flowed into a family, a town, and a Black Cherokee economic network that reached far beyond his own fences.

CHAPTER 11

Zachariah "Zack" Foreman Sr.: A Wealth Case Study

If you want to see the Black Cherokee ledger at work in one life, you can start with Zack Foreman.

Not the legend.
Not the shorthand.
The man.

Born enslaved in the Cherokee Nation.
Freed by war and treaty.
Turned loose in a land that was still sorting out who counted and who did not.

By the time his story crests, he is a cattleman, a landowner, and a man who can bargain with a railroad. His success is unusual, but it is not magic. It rests on the same forces this book has been tracing: slavery, emancipation, land access, allotment, and the uneasy promise of Cherokee citizenship for Black people.

This chapter treats his life as a case study in value created, recorded, captured, and defended.

From Enslaved Child to Cherokee Freedman

Zachariah "Zack" Foreman Sr. was born in the Cherokee Nation in the 1840s, in the final decades before the Civil War. He entered the world as property, not as a citizen. His early years unfolded on Cherokee soil that had already been rebuilt once after removal, under a legal system that recognized Black chattel slavery.

When the Civil War came, the Cherokee Nation split. Some factions sided with the Confederacy, others with the Union. The war tore through Indian Territory, burned farms, and scattered families.

For enslaved people like Zack, it opened a crack in the system that had bound them.

The 1863 Cherokee emancipation act and the 1866 treaty with the United States did the formal work. They ended slavery in Cherokee law and recognized former slaves of Cherokee citizens and certain free Blacks, and their descendants, as citizens of the Nation with all the rights of native Cherokees.

Zack stepped through that crack.

On one side of his life:
He had been counted as a line item, valued as property.

On the other side:
He could be counted as a citizen, eligible to claim land and build something of his own.

The gap between those two statuses is where his case becomes important. It shows what could happen when a Black man in the Cherokee Nation had the legal right, at least on paper, to stand on the land he worked.

Starting with Almost Nothing

Freedom did not come with a starter fund.

Like most Freedmen, Zack left slavery with:

- skills in hard work

- knowledge of local land and people

- almost no capital

He did what many Black men did in that era. He hired out. He worked in other people's fields, tended cattle, and took whatever jobs he could find that paid in coin, food, or both.

Unlike in much of the former Confederacy, though, he had another path open to him. As a Cherokee citizen under the 1866 treaty, he could settle on open land in the Nation, clear it, and claim it as his homestead and farm.

At some point in the years after emancipation, he began to do exactly that. Over time, he:

- located land near Lenapah and the surrounding area in what is now northeastern Oklahoma

- cleared and fenced it

- started with a small herd of cattle, likely purchased one or two at a time as his wages allowed

- built a home and outbuildings to support farm and ranch work

Each decision moved him one step away from pure wage labor and one step toward ownership.

Cattle as Moving Capital

In the world Zack lived in, cattle were one of the most flexible forms of wealth.

A cow could:

- feed a family with milk and meat

- produce calves that expanded the herd

- be sold for cash in tight times

- be driven to railheads and shipped to distant markets

A herd was a savings account on four legs.

Building that herd took patience and risk. Drought, disease, theft, and market swings could wipe out years of work. But in a region where land was shifting from communal to allotted, and where cash was scarce, cattle gave a Cherokee Freedmen rancher some breathing room.

Zack built his herd in stages. He used:

- his own labor

- the labor of family and neighbors

- knowledge of local grass, water, and weather

As his herd grew, so did his leverage. A man who could deliver large numbers of healthy cattle at once had something that railroads and buyers further north wanted.

The Railroad Deal

The moment that often stands out in accounts of Foreman's life is his arrangement with a railroad.

By the 1890s, rail companies were cutting across Indian Territory, hungry for right of way. They wanted access to cattle-producing regions and to future town sites. In many cases they negotiated with tribal governments or with the federal government. In other cases, they dealt directly with individuals whose land lay on desirable routes.

Zack saw an opening.

On his land, he agreed to prepare the roadbed for the Kansas City Southern line. That meant:

- grading the ground

- building the base so that rails could be laid

- doing the heavy, dirty work that turned a line on a survey map into a real bed of crushed stone and earth

In return, the railroad agreed to lay the steel.

The result was simple in appearance but powerful in effect. A track ran across or near his land. Cattle could be loaded onto cars much closer to home. Transportation costs dropped. Market access widened. His ranch shifted from a remote producer to a plugged-in supplier.

Economists who have studied Black wealth in Indian Territory note that very few Native Freedmen anywhere managed to turn land into a rail-linked operation. Foreman's deal marked him as exceptional. It also showed how a Black Cherokee citizen could use federal and corporate hunger for right of way to his own advantage.

Wealth in a Hostile System

By the turn of the twentieth century, Zack Foreman had achieved something that most enslaved people could not have imagined in their own lifetimes:

- a substantial herd

- land holdings in an area where many Black and Native families were losing ground

- direct access to the rail network

- recognition by neighbors, newspapers, and officials as a man of means

Contemporary and modern accounts describe him as one of the wealthiest Black men in Indian Territory, a status echoed by later historical work. His success rested on:

- decades of labor

- careful risk taking

- the legal status of Cherokee Freedmen citizenship

- the particular opportunities of a cattle-based economy in a border region

It also unfolded in a hostile environment.

Allotment and the Dawes Rolls were reshaping landownership. Courts and guardians were stripping many Native and Black families of their allotments. White settlers were moving into eastern Oklahoma in greater numbers, backed by new state laws that enforced segregation and often ignored Native sovereignty.

Zack's wealth did not float above this system. It sat inside it. That meant he had to:

- keep his taxes paid

- navigate allotment restrictions and titles

- defend his holdings in courts and councils when necessary

- manage relationships with white officials and neighbors who might resent his success

Every acre he held and every head of cattle he kept was a small act of defiance against the idea that Black people in Indian Territory were destined to be landless laborers.

Family, Community, and Spillover

Wealth in this story is not just a personal balance sheet. It is also what spills into the lives of others.

Foreman's gains rippled outward in several ways:

- **Employment**
  His ranch provided work for Black men who might otherwise have had to hire out to white or non-Cherokee employers at lower wages or under worse conditions.

- **Purchasing power**
  The money he spent on supplies, equipment, and services flowed into nearby towns, including Black businesses and professionals.

- **Example**
  His presence as a successful Black Cherokee rancher gave younger people a model that contradicted both racist stereotypes and narrow expectations.

- **Institutional support**
  Wealthy individuals in Black Cherokee communities often contributed to churches, schools, and civic efforts. Specific records for Zack's giving are scattered, but in a world where formal philanthropy was rare, even consistent tithing or informal contributions could make the difference for a struggling congregation or school.

At the same time, his success could not fully insulate his children and grandchildren from the larger forces at work. As Oklahoma became a state and segregation hardened, Black professionals and landowners everywhere in the region faced new legal and social barriers. The seeds of Greenwood's later rise and destruction were already in the ground.

Limits of the Case

It is tempting to take a story like Foreman's and turn it into proof that anyone could have done the same. That is not what this case shows.

He was not:

- the average Cherokee Freedman farmer

- the typical Black wage worker

- the common outcome of allotment and race in eastern Oklahoma

He was an outlier. That outlier status is the point.

When one Black Cherokee rancher, starting from slavery, can:

- build a major herd

- secure land and defend it through allotment

- bargain directly with a railroad

it tells us that the structure of law and opportunity in the Cherokee Nation did not make Black wealth impossible. It made it difficult and rare.

The fact that most did not reach his level of wealth does not speak to a lack of ability. It speaks to:

- unequal starting points

- discriminatory enforcement of titles and taxes

- the constant risk of violence and legal stripping

- the narrowness of the window in which such success was even possible

Foreman's ledger sits on top of the ledgers of thousands of other Black Cherokees whose work built the roads, fences, and markets he used.

The Foreman Ledger

We can set Zack's life into the same fourfold ledger this book has used throughout.

Value created

- decades of labor that turned raw land into fenced pasture

- a large herd of cattle that supplied regional markets

- roadbed work that brought a rail line onto his land

Value recorded

- his status as a Cherokee Freedman citizen under the 1866 treaty

- allotment and land records that recognized his holdings

- contracts, formal or informal, with a railroad and buyers

Value captured

- personal wealth in land, cattle, and cash

- employment and indirect support for Black workers and nearby communities

- a measure of autonomy in setting prices, choosing buyers, and negotiating terms

Value at risk

- exposure to the same allotment, guardianship, and tax systems that stripped many others of land

- vulnerability to racial hostility in a state turning toward Jim Crow

- the possibility that later generations would not be able to hold onto the same assets under changing law

Zack Foreman's life does not replace the need for statistics or policy analysis. It grounds them. It shows what Black Cherokee wealth looked like up close when it broke through the expected ceiling.

In the next part of the book, we step from his ranch into a wider map. We trace how Black Cherokee labor and enterprise helped lay the groundwork for Black Wall Street in Tulsa, and how the same structures of law and race that shaped his career would collide with Greenwood's dense Black prosperity in 1921.

CHAPTER 12

Black Wall Street's Indian Territory Roots

If you walk Greenwood Avenue in your mind, you might think the story starts in Tulsa.

Brick storefronts.
The Dreamland Theater lit up at night.
The Stradford Hotel standing tall.

But Greenwood did not fall out of a clear sky in 1906. It grew from ground that was already Black, Native, and practiced in the business of survival. The district that people later called **Black Wall Street** was the dense, urban expression of skills and habits that had been tested for decades in Indian Territory.

This chapter traces that line.

From Black Cherokees and other Native Freedmen on communal land,
to all Black towns scattered across the Territory,
to a strip of forty acres along the Frisco tracks that became Greenwood.

From Removal Roads to "Promised Land"

When the Five Tribes were forced west in the 1830s, enslaved and free Black people walked with them. They endured the same winter roads, hunger, and burial mounds that made up the Trail of Tears.

Slavery continued in Indian Territory into the Civil War era. After emancipation and the Reconstruction treaties of 1866, Freedmen in the Cherokee, Creek, and Seminole nations gained, at least on paper, full citizenship and the right to create property by improving land that the Nations held in common.

That legal opening helped Black families build something rare in nineteenth century America. On tribal land, hundreds of Freedmen households:

- claimed farm sites

- built cabins and barns

- raised crops and livestock

- stitched together towns and neighborhoods that were Black and Native at the same time

Historians estimate that by 1900 African American farmers in the combined Oklahoma and Indian Territories owned about 1.5 million acres, valued at roughly eleven million dollars, with many of those holdings rooted in treaty rights and allotments in the Five Tribes.

At the same time, another Black migration flowed in.

Exodusters from states like Mississippi, Texas, and Louisiana came to Kansas and Oklahoma in the late 1800s, fleeing broken Reconstruction and hard Jim Crow. They were drawn by rumors of Oklahoma as a "promised land," supported by Black boosters who dreamed of an all Black state and organized clubs to promote settlement.

The result by 1920 was a landscape that looked nothing like the flat story of "cowboys and Indians." It was:

- Cherokee Freedmen and Creek Freedmen communities on tribal land

- more than fifty identifiable all Black towns and settlements, including Boley, Langston, Rentiesville, and Tatums

- Black sections of mixed towns such as Muskogee, Okmulgee, and Tulsa itself

Greenwood would rise from this network, not apart from it.

All Black Towns as Training Grounds

Before Greenwood was a district, there were Black towns.

Across Indian Territory and Oklahoma Territory, Black settlers and Freedmen built places where:

- Black farmers could own and vote

- Black merchants could open shops

- Black teachers and preachers could hold authority

By one National Park Service count, from 1865 to 1920 African Americans established more than fifty Black towns and settlements in what is now Oklahoma.

Some of these towns sat squarely within Creek and Seminole nations. Others lay in former Cherokee country. All were shaped by three forces this book has already traced:

- land access through treaty and allotment

- entrepreneurship that grew out of farm and ranch work

- the constant need to defend property and life against white hostility

People in these towns ran:

- general stores

- cotton gins and small mills

- livery stables and wagon yards

- boarding houses and cafes

They raised money for schools and churches. They organized mutual aid. They learned to read county tax lists and allotment notices.

When younger people wanted more than a crossroads store could offer, they did not leave those lessons behind. They carried them into larger places like Muskogee, Okmulgee, and, later, Greenwood.

A Black lawyer or pharmacist, raised in a small Freedmen town, might decide that a dense urban district offered more clients and more safety in numbers. Oral histories and later commentary describe exactly that pattern, with professionals leaving scattered Black towns for the emerging Greenwood area that sat just inside the old Cherokee Nation line.

Greenwood did not teach these people how to do business. Indian Territory did.

Oil, Railroads, and Segregated Streets

Tulsa's boom gave Greenwood its location and its fuel.

Oil strikes near Red Fork in 1901 and Glenn Pool in 1905 turned Tulsa from a Creek settlement into a boom town that promoters called the "Oil Capital of the World" and the "Magic City."

Railroads followed oil. Tracks cut across former tribal land, including Cherokee country, linking wells, refineries, and markets. Greenwood's main artery, the strip along Greenwood and Archer, lay just north of the Frisco tracks, at the edge of what had been Cherokee Nation.

This geography mattered.

South of the tracks, white Tulsa businesses grew with oil money. North of the tracks, segregation and law pushed Black residents into a concentrated district.

In 1906, Ottawa W. Gurley, a Black landowner who had first staked a claim in the Cherokee Outlet Land Run, purchased forty acres along the Frisco line in north Tulsa and platted lots to sell only to Black settlers. He opened a rooming house on a dusty trail that he named Greenwood Avenue.

State law finished the sorting.

When Oklahoma entered the Union in 1907, its first legislature rushed to pass Senate Bill One, a Jim Crow statute that segregated public transportation and signaled a wider program of racial separation. Within a few years, Tulsa had become, in the words of one Black attorney who lived through it, "one of the most sharply segregated cities in the country."

White law said that Black dollars were not welcome in many downtown stores and services. So Black dollars circled inside Greenwood.

Oil made Tulsa rich.
Segregation forced Black prosperity to stack up in one place.

Greenwood as a Concentrated Network

By the late 1910s, Greenwood had become a dense node in the larger Black Indian Territory economy.

The district:

- stretched about forty blocks north from Archer Street and the Frisco line

- held thousands of residents, with estimates near ten thousand Black people on the eve of 1921

- contained a packed commercial strip along "Deep Greenwood," lined with one-, two-, and three-story brick buildings

Inside those buildings, survey reports and local histories list:

- barbershops and beauty parlors

- restaurants, cafes, and confectioners

- meat markets and grocery stores

- clothing and dry goods shops

- tailors, cleaners, and a photography studio

- a drug store and medical and dental offices

- the Dreamland Theater and other entertainment halls

- hotels, including the Gurley Hotel and the Stradford Hotel

- a hospital, library branch, post office substation, and numerous churches

Booker T. Washington visited the district and, impressed by the concentration of Black enterprise, called it the "Negro Wall Street of America." By the 1920s that phrase had softened into "Black Wall Street," and Greenwood's reputation spread far beyond Oklahoma.

Look beneath the storefronts and you can see the familiar patterns from earlier chapters:

- cattle and farm money from Indian Territory flowing into town

- skills in carpentry, blacksmithing, and dressmaking that had been honed on allotments and Native Freedmen farms

- church and lodge networks from Native Freedmen communities feeding members and tithes into urban congregations

When Buck Colbert Franklin, a lawyer from the Black town of Rentiesville, moved his practice to Greenwood in early 1921, he was following a path other had already set: out of small Native Freedmen communities, into a dense district where Black wealth and Black need sat side by side.

Black Cherokee and Creek Freedmen in the Mix

Greenwood was not a "Cherokee town" in any narrow sense. Its residents came from many backgrounds:

- Black migrants from the Deep South

- Black residents of all Black towns like Boley and Langston

- Native Freedmen and their descendants from Creek, Cherokee, and other tribal nations

- mixed families with Native, African, and European ancestry

Even so, the Cherokee Nation is not absent from the map.

The district lay just inside old Cherokee country. It sat alongside rail and road lines that had been used for years by Cherokee Freedmen and other Native Freedmen moving stock and goods. Oral history in Oklahoma remembers that professionals from scattered Black towns came into Greenwood because it was, in the words of one commentator, "really in the Cherokee Nation just barely," and because that border region collected wealth and opportunity.

Black Cherokees and their kin arrived with:

- experience managing cattle herds and land under treaty-based rules

- knowledge of allotment law and the tricks used to strip Black families of land

- ties to people like Zack Foreman, whose ranching success showed what could be done when a Cherokee Freedman made the most of land and rail access

In Greenwood, those experiences translated into:

- Black law practices that served clients with allotment and title problems

- Black real estate deals, where men like J. B. Stradford bought lots and resold them to Black settlers to keep land in Black hands

- investment habits that treated a row of brick buildings as a new kind of fence line

The district did not erase tribal identities, but it did layer them into a shared urban struggle against the same forces that had haunted Indian Territory for decades: dispossession, white mobs, and legal erasure.

Workdays and Paychecks

Greenwood's reputation as Black Wall Street can obscure a hard fact. Most adults in the district were not business owners.

They worked as:

- maids and cooks

- chauffeurs and gardeners

- day laborers and porters

- service workers in white Tulsa homes and workplaces

A report prepared for the state's commission on the 1921 violence notes that the majority of Greenwood's adults worked long hours in menial jobs for white employers, largely barred from higher wage positions in oil and manufacturing. It was their paychecks, earned under harsh conditions, that built Greenwood's brick and mortar.

Because segregation blocked them from spending freely in white districts, those wages piled up in Black owned stores, churches, and banks on Greenwood Avenue.

In that sense, Greenwood's economy worked the same way Black Cherokee economies had worked on a smaller scale:

- Black labor created value in white and Native enterprises

- discrimination blocked access to many outside markets and goods

- Black communities responded by building parallel institutions that captured part of the value at a second step

128

The difference in Greenwood was density.

Dozens of Black enterprises sat within a few blocks, feeding one another's cash flow, sharing customers, and offering a visible alternative to white supremacy. That visibility would later draw fire.

Ledger of the Roots

If we pull back and look at Greenwood's origins through the ledger lens, the columns look like this.

Value created

- Black and Native labor that cleared and improved land in the Cherokee, Creek, and other nations

- Freedmen farms, all Black towns, and rural businesses that trained a generation of Black entrepreneurs and professionals

- oil production and rail development around Tulsa that raised regional demand for services

Value recorded

- Reconstruction treaties that recognized Freedmen as citizens with access to tribal land in common

- Dawes allotment records that turned communal land into individual parcels, including Black owned tracts

- town plats and deeds for Greenwood lots sold to Black buyers, especially the forty acre purchase by Gurley north of the Frisco tracks

Value captured

- Black families who used treaty rights, allotments, and small town enterprises to gain initial land and savings

- Greenwood merchants, landlords, and professionals who transformed wages from menial jobs into capital for Black owned buildings and businesses

Value at risk

- Black and Native landholdings exposed to allotment related fraud, tax sales, and racial violence

- a concentrated Black business district whose very success in a Jim Crow city made it a target for white resentment

- a mixed Black, Native and US Freedmen heritage that federal and state record systems tried to flatten into separate racial categories

Greenwood was not a miracle that appeared from nothing in 1906. It was the visible tip of a much larger structure that began with removal roads, treaty clauses, and cleared fields in Indian Territory.

That is why the destruction of Greenwood in 1921 was not just a local riot. It was another chapter in a long series of economic interruptions that hit Black people tied to the land and law of the Five Tribes.

The next chapter turns directly to that destruction. We look at how the burning of Greenwood functioned as an act of wealth erasure, not only in Tulsa but across the wider network of Black Cherokee and Freedmen economies that had fed the district from the beginning.

CHAPTER 13

Rebuilding After Erasure

On the morning of June 1, 1921, Greenwood's numbers did not make sense anymore.

The ledger of the district had been written in buildings and inventory and careful notes.
Brick walls.
Business signs.
Black ink on lined paper.

By afternoon, the account was written in smoke.

Flames moved from roof to roof.
Safe doors buckled.
Records turned to ash or scattered in the street.

By the time Oklahoma's National Guard restored a kind of order, more than thirty blocks of Black Tulsa lay in ruins. Contemporary and later investigations estimate that at least 1,200 homes were destroyed, along with dozens of businesses, churches, and schools, in a compact district roughly two miles long and several blocks wide. Property damage for Greenwood alone has been estimated around 1.5 to 1.8 million dollars in 1921 currency, a conservative figure.

This chapter treats that night and its aftermath as an economic event, not to flatten the human horror, but to keep faith with the book's method. Greenwood's destruction was the sudden interruption of a Black and Black Native economic engine rooted in Indian Territory. Its rebuilding, without real compensation, was an act of collective finance that would echo forward in every debate over reparations and repair.

The Night the Ledger Burned

The immediate story is familiar. An accusation in a downtown elevator. Talk of a lynching. Black men, some of them veterans, went to the courthouse armed to prevent it. White men did the same, backed by police. A shot fired, then more shots, then a white mob surging into Greenwood, looting, burning, and killing as planes flew overhead and dropped incendiaries or fired into the district.

What matters here are the targets.

Mob and deputized men did not only attack people. They attacked:

- the Stradford Hotel and other boarding houses

- offices of Black lawyers, doctors, and dentists

- groceries, cafes, clothing stores, salons, and barbershops

- churches and a hospital

- private homes that held cash, jewelry, furniture, tools, and archives

According to the Oklahoma Commission's 2001 report, at least 1,256 houses were burned, along with churches, schools, businesses, and a hospital.

That count does not capture what really died in the smoke:

- account books that recorded loans and debts

- deeds and lease contracts kept in back rooms

- personal papers that proved family lines and property claims

- inventory lists used to set insurance coverage and tax values

If you want a single image for that night as an economic event, it is not only the flames in the sky. It is a drawer open on the floor in a burned office, papers scattered and half burned, numbers no longer attached to anything solid.

Insurance: Riot Clauses and Closed Doors

Greenwood's business owners and homeowners had done what every bank and county official told them to do.

They bought insurance.

Many policies covered fire. Many property owners, Black and white, paid their premiums in good faith. After the massacre, more than one hundred policyholders filed lawsuits against their own insurers or the city, seeking payment for buildings and stock that had been reduced to ash. In total, Tulsans filed more than 1,400 lawsuits seeking over four million dollars in compensation for massacre related losses.

The companies said no.

City leaders and insurers labelled the attack a "riot." That single word unlocked a clause in many policies that excluded coverage for damage "caused directly or indirectly by riot, civil commotion, or insurrection." Courts upheld the exclusions. With rare exceptions, only white claimants, such as a white shop owner who lost guns taken from his store, received any payment.

For Black families and business owners, this meant:

- no insurance checks to rebuild stores or homes

- no payouts to cover lost inventory or furnishings

- no recognition from the companies they had trusted

The insurance denials did more than block money. They reclassified the massacre in law and in the public mind. Calling Greenwood's destruction, a "riot" shifted blame away from the organized white violence that caused it and turned the event into something like an act of God for which no one, and certainly no corporation, owed repair.

From the ledger angle, the sequence looked like this:

- premiums paid into the insurance system over years

- mass loss event triggered

- payouts largely refused on a technical label

- value created by Black policyholders transferred upward into company reserves and shareholder accounts instead of back into Greenwood

It is one of the clearest examples in this book of value created and value captured coming apart.

City Hall and the Second Theft

Insurance refusals were the first financial betrayal. City policy was the second.

Immediately after the massacre, Tulsa officials and business interests saw opportunity in the rubble. They proposed new fire ordinances and building codes that would have effectively prevented Black residents from rebuilding on their own land. One plan envisioned turning the burned district into an industrial zone or a rail corridor, forcing Black residents to relocate.

Black lawyers, including Buck Colbert Franklin and A. J. Smitherman, fought back. They challenged the new ordinances in court. They argued that the city could not use its police powers to take Black land through regulation after failing to protect it from white violence. Eventually, the Oklahoma Supreme Court struck down Tulsa's harshest rebuilding restrictions, clearing the way, legally, for Black property owners to reconstruct on their original lots.

What the city did not do was just as important:

- it provided no broad public compensation to Black residents for the destruction

- it did not prosecute white leaders and participants in any way that would yield restitution

- it did not rebuild Greenwood's infrastructure at public expense

So Black Tulsans faced a bitter set of facts:

- their district had been destroyed with the tacit or active involvement of public officials

- their insurance claims had been denied using riot clauses

- the only thing the city now offered was new obstacles

City plans to rezone the area were a second attempt to extract value. If those plans had succeeded, they would have transformed Black owned lots, some held by Native Freedmen descendants and other Black families with ties to Indian Territory, into land for white-controlled industry.

The courts blocked the most extreme version of that second theft. They could not force Tulsa to write checks.

Rebuilding With Bare Hands

What came next is easy to celebrate and easy to misunderstand.

Within a few years of the massacre, Greenwood stood again.

Film footage shot between 1925 and 1928 by Reverend Solomon Sir Jones shows busy streets, newly built brick structures, and a district that, while smaller and scarred, had regained much of its commercial life.

A Tulsa Historical Society and Library summary notes that Greenwood residents rebuilt their homes and businesses "without meaningful assistance from the city, state or federal governments."

That fact carries weight.

Rebuilding meant:

- salvaging bricks and lumber from ruins

- camping in tents and shacks through winters

- borrowing money at harsh terms from whatever sources would lend

- pooling church and lodge funds to finance reconstruction

- working double shifts, laboring by day and rebuilding by night

In some cases, Black property owners who had lost buildings but managed to hold onto land used their lots as collateral. They signed new mortgages in a landscape where racial discrimination made fair credit almost impossible. Every new building carried with it the risk of foreclosure if business conditions shifted or another downturn hit.

From the ledger side, Greenwood's reconstruction turned:

- stored family wealth

- mutual aid funds

- future earnings pledged through debt

into replacement buildings and businesses.

Unlike white neighborhoods destroyed by floods or earthquakes, Greenwood received no major infusion of outside capital. There was no equivalent of a Marshall Plan. The district was left to self-finance its own recovery after one of the worst racially motivated property destructions in United States history.

The result is a hard paradox. Greenwood's recovery showed extraordinary Black financial discipline and solidarity. It also locked a second layer of loss into place, because capital that might have gone into expansion, diversification, or savings had to be spent just to get back to where the district had already been.

Record Loss and Legal Shadows

When buildings burn, the flames do not discriminate between cash and records.

In the months and years after 1921, Greenwood residents trying to rebuild or pursue legal claims ran into a quieter kind of damage:

- burned deeds and mortgage papers

- destroyed business ledgers

- missing insurance contracts and correspondence

- lost personal records that proved births, marriages, and family relationships

Archival work for the Tulsa Race Riot Commission and later research show that many damage claims relied on sworn statements and witness testimony because supporting documents had gone up in smoke. The Commission identified 193 insurance claims from Greenwood totaling about 1.8 million dollars in alleged losses. Converting that to late 1990s or 2020s dollars gives roughly 27 to 32 million dollars, but even that adjustment captures only a fraction of what would have accumulated had Greenwood's assets remained intact and grown.

For Black Cherokee families and other Native Freedmen descendants whose businesses and homes stood in the district, record loss had additional consequences:

- allotment papers kept at home could be destroyed, making it harder to prove title later

- probate records for estates and informal arrangements between relatives might be lost, opening the door to disputes and predatory claims

- contracts that documented debts owed to Black merchants could vanish, turning receivables into uncollectible memories

The massacre thus did double damage to the ledger. It removed assets and removed evidence. It also erased some of the paper trail that connected Greenwood's prosperity back to Indian Territory land claims, Black entrepreneurship, and Native Freedmen allotments.

Later lawyers and descendants would find themselves trying to reconstruct those connections from fragmentary records scattered across county offices, federal archives, and personal collections.

The Long Shadow: Wealth That Never Compound

Economists and historians have tried to quantify what the massacre cost in long term terms.

An analysis prepared for the Joint Economic Committee of Congress estimates that the Tulsa Race Massacre destroyed at least 27 million dollars in Black property in today's money and contributed to lower home ownership, occupational status, and net worth among Black Tulsa residents compared to whites in the decades after 1921.

A Brookings Institution review of the massacre's cost emphasizes that destruction of homes, businesses, and institutions not only wiped out existing assets, but also cut off future returns on those assets. The report notes that more than 1,200 homes were destroyed and that all but one of the more than 100 insurance lawsuits were denied.

Think of one Greenwood block before 1921.

- building shells largely paid off

- businesses expanding inventory

- upstairs apartments rented for regular income

If left alone, that block might have produced:

- rental income for decades

- profits reinvested into new ventures

- education funds for children and grandchildren

- charitable giving to churches, schools, and mutual aid

Instead, the massacre:

- erased the buildings

- pushed owners into new debts

- reduced their ability to send children to college or expand enterprises

- shortened the time horizon of investment, because people had seen how fast everything could be taken

For Blacks and Native Freedmen descendants tied to Greenwood, this meant that the wealth engine built on generations of labor in Indian Territory never had the chance to fully compound.

The massacre also sent a signal beyond Tulsa. It showed other Black communities that visible, concentrated prosperity could make you a target, especially when state and local officials were either sympathetic to white mobs or unable to restrain them.

Rebuilding, Then Undermined Again

Even after the physical rebuilding of the 1920s, Greenwood's economy did not return to its former trajectory.

Federal and local policies in the mid twentieth century hit the district again:

- redlining by banks and federal housing programs made it harder for Black residents to obtain fair mortgages

- urban renewal projects and highway construction carved through north Tulsa, including parts of Greenwood, undercutting property values and displacing residents

- eminent domain was used to take homes and lots at prices below market value, consolidating land into public and institutional hands that did not always serve Black community needs

A Brookings analysis notes that Greenwood "rebuilt itself after the race massacre without help from the government, only to be consistently targeted in subsequent decades by policies such as redlining, federal highways that carved through the neighborhood, and eminent domain that took people's homes for less than market value."

In other words, the massacre was not a single, isolated interruption. It was the first in a series of state shaped blows:

- 1921: mob violence with state complicity

- 1920s: self-financed rebuilding

- mid-century: policy driven undercutting of land and business values

For families whose roots ran back to Black communities, Native Freedmen allotments, and Indian Territory ranching, these later policies looked like a new form of dispossession. Land that had once been tribal, then allotted, then concentrated in a Black business district, was now being sliced up again under federal and city plans.

The Greenwood Ledger

We can now place the destruction and rebuilding of Greenwood into the four-column ledger used throughout this book.

Value created

- decades of Black and Black Native labor in Indian Territory that built the skills, savings, and networks which fed Greenwood

- Greenwood's own dense business district by 1921: more than a thousand homes, nearly two hundred businesses, churches, schools, and professional offices

Value recorded

- property valuations and tax rolls that documented Black owned assets before 1921

- insurance policies that are purported to cover fire losses

- damage claims totaling around 1.8 million dollars in 1921 currency, filed with insurers and the city

Value captured

- before 1921: Black families and businesses in Greenwood were capturing more of the value created by their labor than almost anywhere else in the region

- after 1921: insurance companies, speculators, and state backed projects captured gains by denying claims, acquiring property cheaply, and directing infrastructure in ways that served non-Black interests

Value destroyed or frozen

- millions of dollars in Black property burned in a matter of hours

- legal evidence lost in the fire, making it harder for descendants to prove claims

- the compounding potential of Black wealth in Tulsa was cut off, with long term impacts on home ownership, income, and educational attainment

Greenwood's story is not an aside in Cherokee or Black Cherokee economic history. It is one of the clearest examples of what happens when Black and Black Native prosperity, rooted partly in treaty rights and allotments, collides with racist violence and structural denial. It shows that even when communities self-finance their way back from disaster, the ledger never fully recovers what was taken.

In the next part of this book, we return to the broader map. We look at the patterns that run from slave labor in the eighteenth-century Cherokee Nation to Greenwood's fires, then forward into present debates over citizenship, recognition, and the unfinished ledger of repair.

CHAPTER 14

Follow the Money

If you pull back from the details of this story and look at it from the ceiling, you see less of the individual faces and more of the currents.

Slaves counted next to cattle.
Allotment parcels lined up on maps.
Oil checks cashed in Tulsa.

Money moves.
The question this chapter asks is simple.

When Black people in and around the Cherokee Nation created value, where did that value go.

Not in theory. In practice.

Who wrote it down.
Who captured it.
Who lost it.

The answer is not the same in 1809, 1866, 1902, and 1921, but the pattern that runs through them is steady enough to name.

The Four Columns

All through this book, the story has turned on a simple ledger with four columns:

1. Value created

2. Value recorded

3. Value captured

4. Value denied or redirected

Chapter by chapter, we filled those columns with:

- enslaved Black labor on Cherokee farms and building sites

- fixed improvements left behind at removal

- forced migrations where people moved and land did not

- Black citizenship written into a treaty and then fought over

- Cherokee Freedmen schools and payrolls built from public money

- Outlet leases and sales that turned communal land into paper

- allotment parcels that attached unequal rules to different citizens

- Black Cherokee ranchers and merchants who turned skill into capital

- Greenwood, dense and bright, and then Greenwood in ashes

Now we can stack those ledgers and read the long pattern.

Value Created

Across almost three centuries of Cherokee history, Black people in this story did certain things again and again.

Under slavery

- Cleared thousands of acres of land in the old Nation in the East and in Indian Territory, turning forest and prairie into fields.

- Worked in agriculture, growing corn, cotton, and livestock at scales that fed households and supplied export markets. Historians of Cherokee slavery, such as Theda Perdue and Tiya Miles, describe slave-based plantations that produced substantial surpluses and supported mills, ferries, and merchant ventures.

- Built houses, ferries, mills, and brick public buildings with their hands and skills.

Under emancipation and Reconstruction

- Cleared and improved new lands in Indian Territory under Freedmen citizenship, building small farms and communities that raised both subsistence crops and saleable goods. Scholars of the Reconstruction treaties emphasize that Cherokee, Creek, and Seminole Freedmen used treaty backed land access to reach rates of farm and home ownership higher than many Black Southerners locked into sharecropping.

- Staffed and attended schools that turned tax and treaty dollars into human capital.

Under allotment and statehood

- Developed allotted tracts, often with Black households doing the full work of fencing, planting, and building on their parcels.

- Worked as skilled and unskilled labor on roads, rail lines, and in towns as eastern Oklahoma urbanized.

- Created businesses, from small shops to ranches of regional scale, that linked rural production to rail and city markets. Studies of Black enterprise in Oklahoma point to men like Zack Foreman and to clusters of Black businesses in towns such as Muskogee and Tulsa as the visible proof of this work.

In Greenwood

- Turned wages from service and industrial jobs in white Tulsa into capital for Black owned buildings, theaters, hotels, stores, and professional offices.

- Circulated money within a dense Black district so that each paycheck supported multiple Black enterprises before it left. Local and state reports on pre-1921 Greenwood count well over a hundred businesses, a hospital, a library, churches, and nearly thirteen hundred homes in the district.

Value creation is not the mystery in this story. Black people created value at every step, often at higher intensity and with fewer protections than their neighbors.

Value Recorded

The second column is where the trouble starts.

At every stage, records were kept. The question is what those records were designed to see.

Slavery records

- Federal and Cherokee surveys in 1809 and 1835 counted enslaved Black people as "negro slaves," listed in tables next to livestock and houses, with average values assigned. One early nineteenth century agency report valued 583 enslaved people at about 300 dollars each, several times the value of a typical log house.

- Estate inventories, bills of sale, and court dockets listed enslaved men, women, and children by first name, rough age, and price. They rarely recorded family ties, skills beyond basic labels, or any measure of their own claims.

These records captured Black people as assets, not as participants.

Treaty and claims records

- The Treaty of New Echota and the 1838 claims process recorded Cherokee improvements in the East in dollar terms, but under pressure and often at discounted values. Black labor appears in those records only as part of the value of buildings and cleared land.

- The 1866 treaty recorded Cherokees' obligation to treat Freedmen as citizens with the same rights as native Cherokees. That clause is one of the few places in official law where Black people appear explicitly as rights holders, not property.

Allotment and enrollment records

- Dawes Rolls and Cherokee agreements turned citizens into names in categories: "by blood," "Freedman," "intermarried." Those labels would later control restrictions, taxation, and the ease with which land could be taken or held.

- Allotment jackets recorded parcels assigned to each enrollee, but also leases, guardianships, tax problems, and sales, often with Black and Native owners treated as "incompetent" in ways that justified outside control.

Business and tax records

- City directories, newspapers, and tax rolls in places like Muskogee and Tulsa recorded Black entrepreneurs and property owners, but often incompletely. Men like Zack Foreman show up in a scattering of entries that only hint at the scale of their operations.

- Greenwood's pre-1921 property valuations and insurance policies listed buildings and inventory, but those same records became instruments for denial when "riot" clauses were invoked after the massacre.

The pattern is that records routinely captured:

- Black bodies as property

- Black work as part of someone else's asset

- Black claims only when written into treaties, lawsuits, or the occasional business license

Even then, documents that would have helped Black families defend their claims were fragile or easily ignored.

Value Captured

The third column asks a blunt question.

Who walked away with the gains.

Slaveholding Cherokees and white neighbors

- In the slave era, a small class of Cherokee planters held most of the Nation's enslaved people and improved land. They used Black labor to increase their land under cultivation from levels close to subsistence up to averages several times larger than non-slaveholders, then turned that surplus into cash crops and diversified businesses.

- When removal came, white states and settlers captured the long-term value of former Cherokee land in the East through cotton, timber, mining, and town building, while paying well below market value for the land and improvements.

Cherokee planter class in Indian Territory

- After resettlement, slaveholding families again used enslaved labor to rebuild faster than non-slaveholders. They captured the benefits of salt works, mills, ferries, and large farms that stood on land cleared and maintained by Black people.

- Even after emancipation, the same families often converted their head start in land and capital into positions in new markets, including cattle and town development.

The United States and speculators under allotment

- Allotment and related statutes allowed the federal government to declare surplus lands, open them to non-Indian settlement, and remove restrictions from many individual parcels. That process turned large parts of tribal land bases into white owned property. Legal scholars of Oklahoma land titles have traced how county courts, guardianship systems, and tax sales combined to transfer many Black and Native allotments into white hands.

- Oil development in eastern Oklahoma often rested on leases and rights carved out of allotted lands, with a disproportionate share of the profits captured by non-Native firms.

Insurance companies and city government in Tulsa

- After 1921, insurance companies collected years of premiums from Greenwood property owners, then denied almost all claims by labeling the massacre a riot. The companies kept reserves that would otherwise have flowed back into Black rebuilding.

- City and state governments provided no broad compensation for the destruction, yet later used public power to run highways and urban renewal projects through the same neighborhoods.

Black capture, limited and hard won

None of this means Black people never captured value. They did, particularly when:

- Freedmen citizenship gave access to communal land

- allotments could be held over generations

- schools and churches turned public funds into skills and networks

- ranchers, merchants, and professionals built enterprises that survived for a time

The point is that Black capture required constant defense against systems built to route gains elsewhere.

Value Denied and Redirected

The fourth column is where the ledger shows its teeth.

At each turn, you can see how structures of law and violence redirected or froze value that Black Cherokees and other Black people had created.

- Under slavery, Black labor produced the basis of wealth for Cherokee planters and southern neighbors without wages or capital of their own.

- Under removal, the land those Black people had cleared remained in the East, while they were marched west and forced to rebuild from near zero.

- Under Reconstruction, Cherokee Freedmen were promised equal rights in treaties, yet faced internal political moves to limit their access to per capita payments, schools, and public contracts.

- Under allotment, "Freedmen" categories on the Dawes Rolls were used to justify different restriction and taxation rules that left many Black landowners more exposed to tax sales and predatory guardianship than their "by blood" neighbors.

- Under Jim Crow and oil boom capitalism, Black prosperity in Greenwood was first confined by segregation and then violently targeted. The refusal of insurance payouts and public restitution froze a massive loss in place.

Every time a farm was lost in a tax sale because an allotment shifted from restricted to unrestricted status, every time a Cherokee Freedmen family was left off a payment roll, every time a Greenwood business owner was told that a riot clause erased their policy, value shifted on the books from one side of the ledger to the other.

From Black households and communities
to corporations, white settlers, and state accounts.

Who Writes the Ledger

There is another pattern hiding in plain sight.

The people who wrote the rules of the ledger, and who held the pen for many of its entries, were rarely the same people who did the heaviest work.

- In the slave era, the Cherokee planter class wrote national laws that defined slavery, citizenship, and property, while Black people had no formal voice in council.

- During allotment, Congress and federal commissioners drafted agreements and statutes that reshaped tribal land and citizenship, often over Native objections, and with little direct representation for Native Freedmen.

- In Tulsa, white city leaders and insurers set the terms that converted a massacre into a "riot" to block claims, then tried to use zoning and fire rules to seize burned land.

Black Cherokees and other Black people in this story did get their hands on the pen at key moments:

- applying for and defending citizenship under the 1866 treaty

- serving on school boards and as teachers in Cherokee Freedmen schools

- signing contracts with railroads and buyers

- filing lawsuits after Greenwood burned

Those moments matter. They show that the ledger is not entirely closed. But they also show how costly it has been to force even small corrections.

Defense Strategies

Faced with this tilted ledger, Black communities did not just endure. They developed ways to defend and redirect value.

- **Land claims**
  Cherokee Freedmen invoked treaty language to secure homesteads and allotments in the Cherokee Nation and other tribes. Some families held those lands through allotment, statehood, and beyond, creating pockets of Black landownership that survive today.

- **Education**
  Cherokee Freedmen schools and Black teachers turned limited public funds into literacy and numeracy that allowed Black citizens to read contracts, track taxes, and argue in court. That human capital made later legal challenges and businesses possible.

- **Entrepreneurship and circulation**
  Black Cherokee ranchers, merchants, and professionals created enterprises that kept a greater share of Black spending inside Black hands, from rural trading posts to Greenwood's brick storefronts.

- **Mutual aid and institutions**
  Churches, lodges, and benefit societies pooled small contributions to cover emergencies, funerals, and shortfalls, softening the impact of shocks that might otherwise have forced land or asset sales.

- **Legal action**
  Black lawyers and allies challenged discriminatory ordinances, predatory guardianships, and some unjust tax sales,

sometimes winning protections that helped whole neighborhoods.

These strategies did not equalize the ledger, but they slowed and sometimes reversed the outward flow.

Reading the Ledger Today

What does it mean to "follow the money" in a story like this.

It means recognizing that:

- The inequalities we see in Cherokee citizenship debates, in Black wealth levels in eastern Oklahoma, and in the condition of Greenwood today are not accidents or pure personal outcomes. They are the result of structured transfers of value over time.

- Treaties, allotment statutes, insurance contracts, and zoning ordinances are not dry texts. They are instruments that either recognize and protect the value Black people created, or erase and redirect it.

- Any honest conversation about repair, whether framed as restitution, policy change, or institutional reform, has to account for both the work done and the value lost.

The ledger of Black Cherokee life will never balance perfectly, because some losses cannot be priced:

- ancestors whose labor can only be estimated

- languages and rituals altered by removal and slavery

- lives lost on the Trail, in the Civil War, in the 1921 fires

What can be counted, and must be, are the patterns that remain visible on paper:

- the acres cleared

- the farms and businesses built

- the payments denied

- the assets stripped

Following the money shows that the story of Black Cherokees is not just a story of identity or recognition. It is a story of debt owed and wealth moved.

In the next chapter, we take this one step further. We build a Black Cherokee economic atlas. Instead of only years and laws, we map places and networks: river crossings, town squares, school sites, ranches, and city blocks that, taken together, show how wide and deep this ledger runs across the land.

CHAPTER 15

A Black Cherokee Economic Atlas

If you laid this whole history out on a table, it would not look like a straight line. It would look like a map.

Not just a map of borders and treaties.
A map of work.

Fields where enslaved people hoed corn.
Ferries where Black and Native hands pulled the rope.
Schoolhouses at the crossroads.
Cattle trails that bent toward rail lines.
Brick streets in Greenwood, lit at night.

This chapter is that map in words. It is not a complete atlas. No single volume can be. But it sketches the main routes and clusters so you can see how wide and how connected the Black Cherokee economy has been across time.

Eastern Homelands: Fields, Ferries, and Diamond Hill

The first layer lies east of the Mississippi.

On eighteenth and early nineteenth century maps, the Cherokee homelands spread across parts of what are now Georgia, Tennessee, North Carolina, and Alabama. Inside that space, Black enslaved people worked on:

- plantation style farms near places like Spring Place and along Coosawattee and Etowah river valleys

- ferries that crossed rivers at key points where Cherokee and United States traffic met

- taverns, inns, and trading posts along the Federal Road, a major route that ran through Cherokee country toward the west

One landmark shows this clearly. The house often called Diamond Hill, the Vann plantation at present day Chatsworth, Georgia, was a large brick home built around 1804 for James Vann. Historians Tiya Miles and Theda Perdue note that enslaved Black workers there cleared fields, tended crops, fired bricks, and labored in the house, stables, and mills. The same enslaved workforce also helped build the Cherokee Council House at New Echota and other public buildings near the Cherokee capital.

If you drew an economic map for this period, you would mark:

- river crossings where ferries carried people and goods

- mill sites where grain became flour and lumber

- plantation clusters near mission stations and trading towns

Black labor sat in the center of those nodes, even when the maps and surveys called them "negroes" without names.

The Trail West: Roads as Economic Routes

The Trail of Tears is usually shown as a line of sorrow on a map, an arrow from the East to Indian Territory. It was also an economic route.

Detachments of Cherokees and the people they enslaved traveled along:

- river corridors such as the Tennessee, the Ohio, and the Mississippi

- overland roads through Tennessee, Kentucky, Missouri, Arkansas, and into what is now Oklahoma

On those routes, enslaved Black people:

- cleared fallen trees and brush so wagons could pass

- hunted, cooked, and guarded camps

- tended livestock that survived the journey

Their work stitched a moving supply chain from one homeland to another.

On the atlas, these routes link eastern Cherokee economic nodes to western ones. They mark the human transfer of skills and habits: how to farm bottom land, how to tend cattle, how to build cabins and mills in a new environment.

Indian Territory: Districts, Crossroads, and Salines

In Indian Territory, the Cherokee Nation redrew itself into districts with Tahlequah as capital. A Black Cherokee atlas would shade several kinds of sites.

Government and mission centers

- Tahlequah, with its council house and Supreme Court building, constructed with a mix of Cherokee control and Black labor.

- Park Hill and similar communities, where mission stations, seminaries, and homes of leading families clustered. These were sites where Black domestic and skilled workers lived in the shadow of public and elite buildings.

Saline and mill sites

- Salt works in the western and southern parts of the Nation, where communal springs leased to individuals used enslaved labor before emancipation and then hired labor later.

- Gristmills and sawmills on creeks and rivers, often owned by prominent Cherokee families, where Black workers kept wheels turning. Perdue and other scholars point to these operations as critical nodes in the Nation's move from subsistence to market production.

Freedmen and Black Cherokee settlements

After 1866, Black Cherokee and Freedmen communities spread across the Nation. They rarely appear as bold labels on official maps, but their presence is felt in:

- clusters of churches, often Baptist or Methodist, on the edges of larger towns like Fort Gibson, Tahlequah, Muskogee, and Vinita

- school sites established specifically for Freedmen children under the Nation's public school system

- rural neighborhoods where surnames repeat in census schedules and land records, showing interwoven Black families on adjacent tracts

An atlas of this period would mark small crosses and schoolhouse icons across the Cherokee Nation, showing where Black congregations and classrooms turned land and tax money into community anchors.

Cattle Country: Foreman and the Northern Strip

Moving north in the map, you reach the cattle belt that runs along what is now the Oklahoma-Kansas border.

Here you would mark:

- ranch lands near present day Lenapah, Nowata, and Delaware counties

- rail lines angling toward Kansas City and other Midwestern markets

It is in this zone that Zachariah "Zack" Foreman built his ranch and cut his deal with the Kansas City Southern Railroad. His home place, near Lenapah, becomes a star on the Black Cherokee atlas:

- a Freedman allottee in the Cherokee Nation

- a major Black cattle operation with its own graded rail spur

- a hub that pulled in Black labor and sent out Black raised stock to regional markets

Surrounding him were other Black and Black Native stockmen, not as wealthy but working the same grass. Their places might not be as well documented, but they make up a constellation of smaller dots around the Foreman star, linked by cattle trails and shared knowledge.

Towns of Trade: Muskogee, Fort Gibson, and Nearby Nodes

Drop your finger south and east on the map and you land on Muskogee, Fort Gibson, and nearby towns that developed as mixed trade centers.

By the early twentieth century, Muskogee, sitting at the junction of the Arkansas, Verdigris, and Grand rivers, had become a major commercial hub for Indian Territory and early Oklahoma. Black Cherokees, Creek Freedmen, and other Black residents here:

- ran undertaking businesses, barber shops, small groceries, and professional offices

- worked as porters, domestics, and laborers along riverfronts and rail lines

- used the city as a place to sell surplus from rural farms and to buy manufactured goods

A historical survey of African American Muskogee lists Black undertakers like William Ragsdale, Black physicians and dentists, and other professionals serving a Black population that drew in Freedmen from surrounding tribal lands.

Fort Gibson, an older military post turned town, also functioned as a node where Black labor in freight and service linked rural Cherokee and Creek communities to broader markets.

On the atlas, these towns are junctions:

- goods flow in along rail and river from outside

- produce and stock flow in from Black farms and ranches

- money and information circulate between city and countryside

All Black Towns: Boley, Rentiesville, and Others

Zooming out slightly, you would mark the all-Black towns that dotted Indian Territory and Oklahoma Territory, many of them located in or near former tribal lands.

- Boley in Creek country

- Langston near the old Oklahoma Territory line

- Taft, Clearview, Summit, and Rentiesville in or near the former Muscogee and Cherokee areas

These towns offered:

- Black controlled local government

- Black owned land and businesses

- schools and churches that served as training grounds for future professionals

Rentiesville, for example, is where Buck Colbert Franklin practiced law before moving to Tulsa. Boley became a showcase town, visited by Booker T. Washington, where Black farmers and merchants demonstrated what they could do with land, credit, and cooperation.

On the atlas, the all-Black towns form their own network, connected by roads and mutual aid. Many of their residents had roots in Cherokee, Creek, or Seminole Freedmen communities. They sent sons and daughters into larger markets, including Greenwood, while maintaining family land back home.

Greenwood and North Tulsa: A Dense Node on Old Ground

On the map's western side sits Tulsa. North of the Frisco tracks, in what had been Cherokee country, Greenwood Avenue and its side streets form the tightest cluster of Black capital in the region by 1921.

Here the atlas would draw:

- a thick rectangle for "Deep Greenwood," the main business strip

- radiating blocks of homes up to the Canadian River valley

- anchors such as the Dreamland Theater, Stradford Hotel, Gurley Hotel, churches, and the Black hospital

Arrows would show:

- money flowing in from wages earned in white Tulsa

- remittances and visits arriving from Black towns and rural Cherokee and Creek communities

- cattle and farm income from places like the Foreman ranch finding its way into urban investments

After 1921, the same map would show:

- burn scars across more than thirty blocks

- partial rebuilding in the 1920s

- mid-century highways cutting through the district, re-routing traffic and cracking the Black economic core again

Greenwood is not an isolated symbol on this map. It is the densest point in a mesh of Black Cherokee and Freedmen economic routes.

Schools and Churches as Pins

If you overlaid all these layers, the densest patterns of Black Cherokee economic life would not just be in markets and depots. They would be in schools and churches.

- Freedmen schools in Cherokee districts, sometimes little more than one room buildings on donated land

- church sites in rural settlements, often with cemeteries attached that show family presence over generations

- urban churches in Muskogee, Fort Gibson, and Tulsa that served as both spiritual centers and meeting halls for business, politics, and mutual aid

On the atlas, each of these gets a small mark. Together, they form dense constellations.

You can read them as:

- sites where public and private funds were converted into human capital

- places where offerings and dues became emergency funds, building funds, and sometimes seed money for Black enterprises

- markers of continuity, showing where Black Cherokees and Cherokee Freedmen built institutions that outlasted individual owners and officeholders

Lines That Outlasted Borders

One more thing the atlas shows clearly: borders moved. The routes did not.

- The Cherokee Nation's eastern boundary once stretched through Georgia and the Carolinas, then collapsed under removal.

- The western Cherokee line in Indian Territory later dissolved into county lines when Oklahoma became a state.

- Greenwood's forty-acre core went from Cherokee land to a Black business district inside a segregated city.

Through all those shifts, certain lines stayed active:

- cattle trails bending from Black and Native ranches toward railheads

- wagon roads from Native Freedmen settlements into trade towns

- train routes carrying Black migrants from the Deep South into Oklahoma

- footpaths from allotment farms to local schools and churches

On the Black Cherokee economic atlas, those lines are the veins. They carry value, news, and people in both directions.

Why the Atlas Matters

Laying this history out as a map does a few things that dates alone cannot.

- It shows that Black Cherokee and Cherokee Freedmen economies were not marginal. They sat on rivers, rail lines, and town centers, in the same spaces that drove regional development.

- It makes clear that when land policies changed or violence struck, the damage hit not just individuals, but entire networks. Burning Greenwood was not only the destruction of a district.

It was a blow aimed at a hub in a wider Black and Black Native system.

- It helps explain why present debates over Cherokee citizenship, Native Freedmen rights, and reparations in Tulsa cannot be separated. The same routes and places appear in all three conversations.

Most of all, the atlas reminds us that the ledger in this book is written on the land as much as on paper. Every field a Black family cleared, every ferry that hired Black labor, every Native Freedmen schoolyard, every mile of railroad graded by Black hands, every brick laid in Greenwood, marks a place where value was created.

Whether that value was captured, stolen, or still partly held is the work of the next and last turn of the book.

The conclusion takes this map and this ledger and asks the blunt question they lead to. If we stop treating this as a moral mystery and start treating it as an accounting problem, what does justice look like.

Conclusion

Value Created vs Value Captured

If you strip this story down to its beams, it comes to three sentences.

Black people built value in and around the Cherokee Nation.
The legal and economic systems around them decided where that value would land.
We are still living with the results.

This book set out to treat that story less like a legend and more like a ledger. Not to deny its moral weight, but to ask very clear questions that accountants and auditors ask every day.

What went in.
What came out.
Who held the pen.

What We Saw When We Followed the Money

Across three centuries, the same pattern appeared in different clothes.

- In the eastern homelands, enslaved Black people cleared fields, built houses of brick, and turned Cherokee farms into plantations that could produce export crops. Their value showed up in slave schedules and estate inventories, priced at several times the cost of a log cabin, but always under someone else's name.

- Removal to Indian Territory wiped out much of the fixed asset column for Cherokees. The Nation lost houses, orchards, and mills in the East and had to rebuild in the West. Black labor again did the hardest work: clearing timber, fencing fields, firing bricks for new public buildings in Tahlequah and district centers. The planter class, now on new soil, still recovered fastest because they carried enslaved workers, livestock, and political power with them.

- Emancipation and the Treaty of 1866 finally wrote Black citizenship into law. Freedmen and their descendants were promised "all the rights of native Cherokees" and used that promise to claim land, build farms, and demand schools that their taxes helped fund. Yet council debates and later statutes tried repeatedly to narrow who counted when money and land were at stake, especially in per capita distributions.

- Allotment turned communal land into paper and paper into unequal rules. Rolls split citizens into "by blood" and "Freedmen" categories. Subsequent federal acts tied tax status and sale restrictions to those categories. Many Black allottees found their land unrestricted and taxable earlier than that of their full blood neighbors, which made them easier targets for debt, guardianship, and tax sales.

- Black Cherokees and Freedmen pushed back by building their own economies. They turned allotments into farms, cattle into herds, skills into contracts, and Freedmen schools into human capital that could not be taken as easily as land. Entrepreneurs such as Zack Foreman showed what could happen when a Black Freedman used treaty backed land access and business sense to reach railroads and regional markets.

- Greenwood concentrated those scattered gains into one visible Black business district. Black wages from service work in white Tulsa, Black savings from Indian Territory farms and towns, and Black skills from Freedmen schools and Black colleges all met on Greenwood Avenue. For one brief period, the ledger in that neighborhood tilted toward Black capture more than almost anywhere else in the region.

Then the massacre of 1921 turned that ledger to smoke. Insurers denied claims on technical riot clauses. City leaders blocked serious public compensation. Mid-century highways and redlining later cut through what had been rebuilt. Economists now estimate that tens of millions of dollars in Black property, and a century of compounding gains, never had the chance to grow.

The pattern is not subtle.
Black people created value in each era.
Structures of law and violence decided again and again that much of that value belonged elsewhere.

When the Nation Itself Picks Up the Ledger

There is a new fact in this story that does not fit the old script.

The Cherokee Nation itself has started to talk plainly about enslavement, wealth, and debt. Not as rumor or sidelong apology, but as official work.

In 2017 a federal court in *Cherokee Nation v. Nash* held that the Treaty of 1866 gives Cherokee Freedmen descendants a present right to citizenship that is "coextensive with the rights of Native Cherokees."

In 2021 the Cherokee Nation Supreme Court ruled that this reading is binding and struck blood language from the Nation's laws. The court held that any attempt to change the constitution solely to deny Cherokee Freedmen descendants' citizenship "shall never be law." Soon after, the Nation removed "by blood" restrictions from its constitution and the United States Department of the Interior approved a new charter that guarantees full citizenship for Cherokee Freedmen descendants.

That is a ledger event.
It takes Black people who had been pushed to the margin and writes them back in as full shareholders in the national account.

Then, in 2025 and 2026, the Principal Chief used executive orders to create and then receive a Task Force to Examine the Impact of

Slavery on Cherokee Nation's 19th Century Economy and Infrastructure. The Task Force's final report, issued in January 2026, concludes in clear language that Black chattel slavery:

- provided a distinct economic advantage to slaveholding households

- served as a primary engine for the Nation's transition from subsistence to a more capitalist economy

- played a pivotal role in building national infrastructure, including government buildings and educational institutions

The report also calls for:

- deeper archival research into enslaved people's lives

- a register of structures built with slave labor

- changes in museum interpretation so that slavery and Freedmen history are woven into public stories

Those steps do not change the past. They change what the Nation is willing to put in the "recorded" column.

For Black Cherokees and Cherokee Freedmen descendants, that matters. It means official recognition that their ancestors' unpaid labor built core pieces of Cherokee wealth. It means that any future policy conversation around land, education, or economic development now has an internal document that says plainly: the system had help, and that help has receipts.

Greenwood, Tulsa, and Open Accounts

Outside of tribal politics, Greenwood's ledger is still unsettled.

In 2021 the Oklahoma Commission's earlier findings were paired with national analyses that describe how the massacre decimated more than 27 million dollars of Black property in today's dollars and left lasting scars in home ownership, income, and schooling for Black Tulsans.

Yet courts have repeatedly refused to provide direct legal remedies. In 2024 the Oklahoma Supreme Court dismissed a reparations lawsuit brought by the last known living survivors, closing one of the few remaining judicial paths for direct compensation. Human rights groups describe that refusal as a fresh failure of justice layered on top of the original economic crime.

At the city level, Tulsa's first Black mayor has recently proposed a 100-million-dollar private trust to support descendants of massacre victims and to invest in North Tulsa housing, infrastructure, and scholarships. He has framed it not as full reparations, but as a "road to repair."

Put those moves on the ledger:

- value lost in 1921 and re-lost under mid-century policy

- partial recognition in commissions and scholarship

- little direct restitution through courts

- emerging local efforts to rebuild communities through targeted investment

For Black Cherokees and Cherokee Freedmen descendants who tie their family story to both Indian Territory and Greenwood, the account is still open.

What Justice Looks Like in Accounting Terms

If you look at this history as pure morality, the conclusion is simple. There was wrong. There was courage. There was survival.

If you look at it as an accounting problem, the conclusion is more specific.

Value moved in certain directions. Some of that flow can be traced and, in part, reversed.

Justice in this frame means:

- **Correcting the books inside the Nation**
  Holding firm to the legal recognition that Freedmen descendants are full citizens. Treating their communities as equal priorities in housing, health, education, and economic policy. Making sure allocations from national revenue streams reach Black Cherokee neighborhoods and institutions in real and visible ways, not only in symbolic gestures.

- **Protecting remaining Black and Black Native land**
  Strengthening legal support for families still holding allotment-based tracts or historic Black town properties, including help with probate, clear title, and protection from predatory purchase offers.

- **Investing where value was extracted**
  Channeling new funds into the same places where Black labor built past wealth: Freedmen communities, former Greenwood blocks, Black Cherokee church corridors, and school neighborhoods. Not as charity, but as a form of overdue dividend.

- **Preserving and expanding the record**
  Continuing the work of the 2026 Task Force, but going further: digitizing Freedmen related records, funding community history projects, and ensuring that Black Cherokee stories appear in classrooms, museums, and law schools. Every new document properly described and made public adds another line to the "recorded" column that cannot be easily erased.

- **Reopening conversations about repair beyond the court house**
  Courts in Oklahoma have narrowed formal paths to reparations for Greenwood. That does not prevent tribal

governments, cities, nonprofits, and businesses from acknowledging specific harms and setting up funds, fellowships, and land return programs that meet them. The question is not whether there is legal liability under one narrow statute. The question is whether institutions willing to profit from the old ledger are now willing to help balance it.

Justice here is not a single check or a single apology. It is many small corrections that, taken together, change where value will land for the next generation.

Why the Ledger Is Still Alive

The title of this book is *The Ledger and the Land.*

By now the reason should be clear.

The land matters because it holds the memory of work. Every fence line, every ferry site, every churchyard, every burned block in Greenwood is a page in the story.

The ledger matters because it shows, in ink, what words like "slavery," "citizenship," and "massacre" did in practice. It forces us to ask: when Black hands built this, what happened next in the books.

That question is not historical only. It is present tense.

Every budget passed by the Cherokee Nation, every urban development plan in Tulsa, every grant awarded to digitize Cherokee Freedmen records, every scholarship fund bearing a Greenwood name, is a fresh ledger entry.

The point of following the money backward is not to get stuck in the past. It is to see clearly which way we are facing when we move forward.

If you can look at the long account and say, with a straight face, that nothing is owed, then this book has failed.

If you look at it and see not only loss, but also the hard proof of Black creativity, courage, and persistence inside the Cherokee story, then the ledger has done its other job. It has shown not just what was taken, but what was built that no one could quite kill.

The receipts are still alive.

The question that remains is whether the people and institutions living on that inheritance are finally ready to act like they have seen them.

Epilogue

The Receipts Are Still Alive

Before we close the book, I want to be clear about who I am talking about and how.

In the nineteenth century, the law and the treaties called our people **Cherokee Freedmen**. That was the name for Black men, women, and children who had been enslaved by Cherokee citizens, set free by the Cherokee Emancipation Act and the Treaty of 1866, and recognized in that treaty as citizens of the Cherokee Nation.

By the early twentieth century, those families show up again as **descendants of Cherokee Freedmen**, fighting through allotment, Jim Crow, and Greenwood.

In the present tense, those same families are **Black Cherokees**. They are citizens of the Cherokee Nation. Just as the descendants of U.S. Freedmen are Black Americans, the descendants of Cherokee Freedmen are Black Cherokees.

The names shift because the law shifted. The people did not.

Hold that in your mind while you hold the receipts.

If you have walked with me this far, you are carrying receipts.

Not the kind that crumple in your pocket. The kind that live in your head.

You have names.
You have dates.
You have places.

You know that in 1809 an agent could count enslaved people in Cherokee country and assign them an average price.
You know that in 1838 families listed every peach tree and fence panel they lost on their way out of the East.
You know that in 1866 a treaty promised Cherokee Freedmen and their descendants the same rights as native Cherokees, and that the fight over those words never really stopped.
You know that in 1902 communal land broke into paper, and that some paper was built to tear.
You know that in 1921 more than thirty blocks of Black life burned in Tulsa, and that insurance companies and courts called it a riot and turned their backs.

Those are receipts.

They prove two things at once.

First, Black people in and around the Cherokee Nation have been building value as long as there has been a Cherokee economy to speak of.
Second, somebody else has been trying, again and again, to move that value off our balance sheet.

The receipts are ugly. They are also powerful.

Because once you see them, you cannot pretend the ledger is an accident.

What We Do with the Receipts

A receipt is only paper until somebody decides to act on it.

There are at least four kinds of work ahead, and they belong to different people in different ways.

1. Tribal work

Inside the Cherokee Nation, the receipts point to very specific tasks.

- Protect Black Cherokee citizenship not just as a legal fact, but as a daily practice. That means budget lines, program choices, and leadership pipelines that treat Black Cherokee communities as part of the center, not the edge.

- Put slavery, Cherokee Freedmen, and Black Cherokee life in every serious telling of Cherokee history, not as a footnote at the back of a museum hall. The 2026 slavery impact study is not the last word. It is a floor.

- Study the slave-built sites, mark them, and let Black Cherokees shape how those stories are told on that ground. A building that stood on enslaved labor is a place where repair can start, not just where guilt should sit.

2. City work

For Tulsa and other towns built on Indian Territory's old bones, the receipts demand more than plaques.

- The blocks where Greenwood stood are not empty history. They sit inside living zoning codes, tax zones, and development plans. Every new project in that footprint is a chance to ask, out loud, who lost what here, and how can this choice point some of that value back.

- North Tulsa and other Black neighborhoods need more than remembrance. They need capital at patient terms, land returned or co owned, and safeguards that keep the next wave of renewal from repeating the same game in a different decade.

3. Family and community work

Receipts are also personal.

- Some families reading this will have Dawes numbers, allotment maps, or oral stories that sit in a shoebox or a folder. Bring them out. Scan them. Share them with your elders and your children. The archive grows stronger every time a piece of paper is made legible to more than one pair of eyes.

- Churches, lodges, and community groups can treat their own histories as assets. Meeting minutes, land deeds, old photographs, and cemetery lists are not clutter. They are proof. They show that we were here, that we paid, that we built.

4. Outside work

If you are reading this and you do not come from these communities, the receipts still speak to you.

- They call on you to stop treating Cherokee slavery, Freedmen citizenship, and Greenwood as side stories. They are central to any honest picture of wealth in this region.

- They ask you to look at whatever institution you touch a little more like an auditor. Where did this land, this building, this endowment come from. Who built it. Who was pushed out. What would it mean to acknowledge that with more than a statement.

The Ledger Is Not Closed

It is easy to talk about slavery, removal, allotment, and Greenwood as if they live in a sealed past. The receipts say otherwise.

They show up in:

- county land records that still carry the names of Cherokee Freedmen allottees and the dates their parcels slipped away

- court cases where Black Cherokee citizenship and treaty language are still being argued

- school curriculums that decide whose stories are on the page and whose are extra

- budgets that quietly steer money away from the same neighborhoods that were stripped a century ago

The ledger is not an old book on a dusty shelf. It is the software that still runs in the background.

That is why this project has insisted on talking about value, not just virtue.

People can argue forever about feelings. It is harder to argue with a pattern that shows up across tax rolls, treaties, insurance denials, and court decisions.

When you call something an accounting problem, you are not draining it of emotion. You are saying, this happened, here is the trail, here is the imbalance, and here, in principle, is where repair could begin.

Not Just What Was Taken, But What Survived

If you close this book only angry, you have missed something real.

What survived in this story is not just suffering.

- Black hands built houses in the East and in Indian Territory that still stand, even when their names do not appear on the plaques.

- Cherokee Freedmen took a treaty clause and used it like a crowbar to pry open citizenship for their descendants. Their grandchildren and great-grandchildren stand today as Black Cherokees under that same promise.

- Freedmen schools, held together with thin budgets and thick patience, raised children who became teachers, preachers, lawyers, and ranchers.

- A man born enslaved in the Nation turned cattle and courage into a rail-linked ranch that fed and employed others.

- A burned district pulled itself back into brick and board without the help it was owed.

Those are credits on the ledger.

No amount of theft can erase the fact that people did these things. That they figured out, again and again, how to turn the little they were given into something that fed more than themselves.

The danger now is not that we will forget the harm. It is that we will forget the precision and creativity of the people who lived through it.

The Work After the Last Page

A book ends. The ledger does not.

When you set this down, the question is not whether you agree with every line. It is what you do with the receipts in your hands.

- If you sit in a tribal meeting, a classroom, a courtroom, a city council, carry this history into the room when budgets and laws are on the table.

- If you stand on land that used to be Cherokee communal ground or Greenwood brick, say so. Out loud. Let that truth guide what you build next.

- If you are a Black Cherokee, a descendant of Cherokee Freedmen, know that this account is not charity and not myth. It is a record of work already done and value already earned. You are not asking to be let in. You are asking to be paid what is due and to be trusted with what you have already proven you can build.

The receipts are still alive.
They sit in archives and family Bibles, in treaty texts and burned edges of paper.
They live in streets, fields, and buildings that look ordinary until you know what happened there.

They are waiting for people, and for Nations, who are finally
ready to read them like adults.

Appendix A

Timeline of Money, Law, and Black Cherokee Life

This is not every date. It is a backbone.
Use it as a quick route through the long story the book just walked slowly.

I keep the focus on four things:
land, labor, law, and ledgers.

1700s – early 1800s: Slavery and Market Roads in the East

Late 1700s

- Enslaved Africans and African Americans begin to appear regularly in records of wealthy Cherokee families in the Southeast.

- Why it matters: Black labor becomes part of the Cherokee economy before there is a Cherokee Nation constitution on paper.

Early 1800s

- Cherokee elites adopt plantation style agriculture in parts of present-day Georgia and Tennessee.

- Enslaved Black people clear land, plant cash crops, operate mills, and work river ferries. Historians such as Theda Perdue and Tiya Miles document large slaveholdings at places like Diamond Hill and New Echota.

- Ledger note: Black labor is already being counted as property and used as collateral inside Cherokee society.

1809

- A federal agency report values 583 enslaved people in Cherokee country at about 300 dollars each, compared to 10 to 60 dollars for an ordinary log home.

- Ledger note: on official paper, a Black body is worth several houses. The accounting logic of people as capital is in full effect.

1820s – 1830s: Constitutions, Claims, and Removal

1827

- Cherokee Nation adopts a written constitution. A high share of the men who sign it are slaveholders.

- Why it matters: the same elite that builds a modern style government is deeply invested in slavery as an economic system.

1830

- United States passes the Indian Removal Act. Georgia and other states push hard to seize Cherokee land.

- Ledger note: the outside pressure is about land value as much as it is about power.

1835

- Treaty of New Echota is signed by a small Cherokee faction.

- 1835 census of Cherokees east of the Mississippi records slaveholders and land holdings. Slaveholding households work far more acres on average than non-slaveholders.

- Why it matters: the treaty sets the price for land and improvements in the East. The census shows how much of that improved land rested on enslaved labor.

1838 – 1839

- Trail of Tears. Cherokees and the people they enslave are forced west.

- Many families file 1838 claims listing houses, orchards, fences, and other improvements left behind.

- Ledger note: fixed assets stay in the East. Black and Cherokee people carry only skills, tools, and trauma into Indian Territory.

1840s – early 1860s: Rebuilding with Slave Labor in Indian Territory

1840s – 1850s

- Cherokee Nation rebuilds in Indian Territory.

- Enslaved Black people clear new fields, rebuild salt works, operate ferries, and help construct government buildings in Tahlequah and mission schools in Park Hill.

- Why it matters: the second Cherokee capital is built on the backs of the same people who built the first.

Ongoing 1800s entries

- Bills of sale, runaway ads, and court records in Cherokee and regional papers show active buying, selling, hiring out, and taxation of enslaved people as chattel.

- Ledger note: the Nation's books treat Black people as liquid assets that can be taxed, mortgaged, or auctioned to satisfy debts.

1861 – 1866: Civil War, Emancipation, and Treaty Citizenship

1861 – 1865

- Civil War splits the Cherokee Nation. Different factions ally with Union and Confederate forces. Fighting devastates farms and towns in Indian Territory.

- Black people, free and enslaved, serve as laborers, scouts, and sometimes soldiers with Native and U.S. units.

1863

- Cherokee National Council passes an act that abolishes slavery in the Nation.

- Ledger note: the law changes, but enforcement is uneven until the war ends.

1866

- Treaty of 1866 between the Cherokee Nation and the United States.

- Key clause: former slaves of Cherokee citizens and certain free Blacks, and their descendants, "shall have all the rights of native Cherokees."

- Why it matters: this is the legal birth of Cherokee Freedmen citizenship. That promise is the root of present day Black Cherokee status.

1870s – 1890s: Reconstruction, Freedmen Communities, and Cattle

1870s – 1880s

- Cherokee Freedmen families establish farm communities across the Nation, building cabins, churches, and schools.

- The Nation funds some Freedmen schools as part of its public system, paying Black teachers from tribal revenues.

- Ledger note: a portion of national funds begins to flow back into Black communities in the form of salaries and school buildings.

Late 1800s

- Cattle ranching expands in the northern and western parts of the Cherokee Nation.

- Black Cherokees and Freedmen work as cowhands, teamsters, and small stock owners.

- All Black and Black Indian towns such as Taft, Rentiesville, and others grow nearby, serving as trade and institutional centers.

1890s

- Zachariah "Zack" Foreman Sr., born enslaved in the Nation, has by now built a major cattle operation near Lenapah.

- He arranges with the Kansas City Southern Railroad to grade a roadbed on his land in exchange for track, giving him direct rail access.

- Ledger note: a Black Cherokee citizen uses land, treaty status, and business sense to capture a rare level of wealth and market power.

1890s – 1907: Dawes, Allotment, and New Borders

1893 – early 1900s

- Dawes Commission creates rolls for the Five Tribes.

- Cherokee citizens are sorted into categories: "by blood," "Freedmen," "intermarried."

- Why it matters: these labels later control land restrictions, taxation, and even future citizenship fights.

1902

- Agreement with the Cherokee Nation sets the terms of allotment.

- Each enrolled citizen is to receive land equal in value to 110 acres, with a homestead portion equal in value to forty acres that is temporarily inalienable.

- Ledger note: communal land is converted into individual paper titles. The rules attached to those titles are not equal for everyone.

1907

- Oklahoma becomes a state.

- State constitution and early laws lock in Jim Crow segregation.

- Many restricted allotments begin to shift toward taxable and alienable status under new federal acts. Black and Native landholders become targets for tax sales and guardianship.

1906 – 1921: Greenwood Rises

1906 – 1910s

- O. W. Gurley and other Black landowners plat lots north of the Frisco tracks in Tulsa on former Cherokee land and sell them to Black buyers.

- Greenwood Avenue develops as a Black business district.

- Black residents include migrants from the Deep South, Black town settlers, Creek and Cherokee Freedmen descendants, and other Black Indians.

1910s

- Greenwood, also called Little Africa, grows into a dense Black commercial center with hotels, theaters, doctors, lawyers, cafes, and more than a thousand homes.

- Booker T. Washington visits and calls it the "Negro Wall Street of America."

Ledger note: wages earned in white Tulsa and income from Black farms and ranches flow into Black owned buildings and enterprises on Greenwood Avenue.

1921 and After: Destruction, Rebuilding, and Policy Blows

May 31 – June 1, 1921

- Tulsa Race Massacre.

- White mobs, some deputized by local authorities, invade Greenwood, burning more than thirty blocks, including roughly 1,200 homes, dozens of businesses, churches, and a hospital.

- At least dozens, likely hundreds, of Black residents are killed.

- Property loss in Greenwood alone is estimated in the range of 1.5 to 1.8 million dollars in 1921 money.

1921 – 1920s

- Insurance companies deny almost all claims, citing riot clauses.

- Tulsa officials attempt to pass new building codes and rezoning plans that would have prevented Black residents from rebuilding on their land.

- Black lawyers challenge these moves. Courts eventually strike down the harshest ordinances.

- Greenwood residents rebuild many homes and businesses with their own labor and limited credit, without meaningful public compensation.

Mid 1900s

- Federal housing policies and bank redlining restrict mortgage access for Black Tulsans.

- Urban renewal and highway projects cut through North Tulsa, including parts of Greenwood, displacing residents and depressing property values.

Late 1900s – Early 2000s: Legal Fights and Historical Reckoning

1970s – 1990s

- Cherokee politics continue to argue over the status of Freedmen descendants.

- Amendments and policy choices inside the Nation restrict Freedmen citizenship rights, often tying citizenship to "by blood" language on Dawes Rolls.

1997 – 2001

- Oklahoma establishes the Tulsa Race Riot Commission to investigate the 1921 massacre.

- The Commission's 2001 report documents the scale of destruction and the long-term economic impact, and recommends reparations, which the state does not fully implement.

2000s – 2010s: Courts and Constitutions

2007

- Cherokee Nation voters approve a constitutional amendment linking citizenship to an ancestor listed as Cherokee "by blood" on the Dawes Rolls, effectively excluding most descendants of Cherokee Freedmen.

2017

- Federal court decision in *Cherokee Nation v. Nash* holds that the Treaty of 1866 guarantees Freedmen descendants citizenship "coextensive" with other Cherokee citizens.

- Ledger note: the treaty clause from 1866 is re activated in modern law.

2021

- Cherokee Nation Supreme Court rules that constitutional "by blood" language is void and that Freedmen descendants have a right to citizenship rooted in the 1866 treaty.

- Cherokee Nation removes "by blood" from its constitution.

- United States Department of the Interior approves the new constitution that guarantees full citizenship for descendants of Cherokee Freedmen.

2020s: Task Forces, Trusts, and Open Accounts

2020 – 2024

- The Principal Chief issues Executive Order 2020-05 on equality and later an addendum, calling for examination of historical disenfranchisement, including towards Freedmen descendants.

January 27, 2026

- The Principal Chief's Task Force to Examine the Impact of Slavery on Cherokee Nation's 19th Century Economy and Infrastructure releases its final report.

- Key findings:

    Black chattel slavery gave slaveholding Cherokee households a distinct economic advantage.

    Enslaved labor was central to the Nation's shift from subsistence to a more capitalist economy.

    Slave labor helped build core government and educational structures.

- Recommendations include deeper archival research, a register of slave-built structures, and changes in museum interpretation so that slavery and Freedmen history are fully integrated into Cherokee public history.

Present tense

- Descendants of Cherokee Freedmen stand as Black Cherokees, citizens of the Cherokee Nation whose status is anchored in the 1866 treaty and the 2021 constitution.

- In Tulsa, activists, survivors, and descendants continue to press for reparations and meaningful repair for Greenwood, while new projects experiment with community ownership of land and buildings in the district.

This is the line this book has followed:
from enslaved Black people in the eastern Nation,
to Cherokee Freedmen in Indian Territory,

to Black Cherokees and other Black communities fighting to hold
what they built in Oklahoma.

    The dates here are mile markers.
The real story is in the work that filled the years between them.

Appendix B

Key Figures and Mini-Profiles

These are not the only people who matter in this story. They are anchor points.

Each one shows how a single life can bend a ledger.

James Vann

Cherokee planter, ferry operator, enslaver

James Vann was a wealthy Cherokee leader in the early 1800s whose plantation at Diamond Hill, in present day Georgia, became a symbol of Cherokee "civilization" to white observers. Beneath that image lay a large enslaved workforce that cleared land, tended crops, fired bricks, and served travelers at his inn and ferry.

Vann's wealth rested heavily on enslaved Black labor. He owned more enslaved people than almost any other Cherokee of his time and invested in taverns, mills, and transport routes that linked Cherokee country to broader markets.

In the ledger of this book, Vann represents the Cherokee planter class that used slavery to turn communal land into private capital. His estate shows how early Cherokee wealth was built on an economic system that treated Black people as assets first and people second.

John Ross

Principal Chief, negotiator, slaveholder

John Ross served as Principal Chief of the Cherokee Nation during the crisis over removal. He fought removal politically and legally, then led his people through the Trail of Tears and into reconstruction in Indian Territory.

Ross himself came from a mixed ancestry mercantile family and, like many elite Cherokees of his day, owned enslaved Black people. After removal, he continued to hold enslaved labor and managed properties and political structures that depended on that system.

In this narrative, Ross sits at the intersection of survival and compromise. He defended Cherokee national rights against the United States while maintaining an internal social order that kept Black labor in bondage until the Civil War forced a change. His life reminds us that Native resistance to U.S. dispossession and Native participation in Black enslavement can occupy the same ledger line.

Stand Watie

Confederate general, Cherokee leader, slaveholder

Stand Watie was a prominent Cherokee leader from a slaveholding family who supported the Treaty of New Echota and later became a brigadier general in the Confederate Army.

He owned enslaved Black people before the war and remained committed to a social and economic order that tied Cherokee prosperity to plantation style agriculture. After removal, his family estates in Indian Territory relied on enslaved labor, and records show him buying and selling Black people as chattel.

Watie's prominence in Cherokee and Confederate history shows how deeply slavery and pro-Confederate politics were intertwined among segments of the Nation's elite. On the ledger, he represents the side of Cherokee leadership that chose to align with the slaveholding South and fought to preserve a system that treated Black people as movable wealth.

Cherokee Freedmen

From property to citizens on paper

"Cherokee Freedmen" is not one person. It is a legal name attached to thousands.

These were Black men, women, and children who had been enslaved by Cherokee citizens, as well as certain free Blacks living in the Nation, who became free under Cherokee law and the Treaty of 1866. That treaty promised that Freedmen and their descendants "shall have all the rights of native Cherokees."

These people:

- rebuilt farms and communities after the Civil War

- claimed land and allotments inside the Cherokee Nation

- sent their children to Freedmen and public schools

- fought in councils and courts to defend the rights the treaty promised

In the present tense, their descendants are Black Cherokees. Their story is the spine of this book. They show how Black labor that once appeared as property on a slave schedule later reappeared as citizenship claims, land titles, and court cases.

Zachariah "Zack" Foreman Sr.

Black Cherokee rancher, rail negotiator, employer

Zack Foreman was born enslaved in the Cherokee Nation in the 1840s and became free under Cherokee emancipation and the Treaty of 1866. Using his status as a citizen and his knowledge of the land, he built a major cattle operation near what is now Lenapah, in northeastern Oklahoma.

Foreman:

- acquired and improved land in former Cherokee country

- built a herd large enough to supply regional markets

- negotiated directly with the Kansas City Southern Railroad, agreeing to prepare roadbed on his land in exchange for a line of track

That deal gave him direct rail access from his ranch to outside markets and marked him as one of the wealthiest Black men in Indian Territory.

On the ledger, Foreman is a case study in Black Cherokee wealth building. He shows what could happen when a Freedman citizen had access to land, skill, and a willingness to treat cattle, contracts, and railroads as tools, not as closed doors.

Black Cherokee Teachers and School Builders

Human capital makers

Many of the names of Black Cherokee teachers have been lost or scattered in school board minutes and pay rolls, but their impact is everywhere in the story.

These were Black men and women who:

- ran Freedmen schools in rural districts

- taught reading, writing, arithmetic, and civic knowledge in one room buildings

- often worked for low pay and with minimal supplies

- helped parents navigate allotment notices, tax bills, and petitions

Their classrooms turned treaty promises and tax revenues into skills that their students carried into farming, preaching, law, business, and community leadership.

In the ledger, these teachers converted public funds into human capital that could not be seized as easily as land. They are the quiet engine behind later Black Cherokee professionals and entrepreneurs.

Ottawa W. Gurley

Land investor, Greenwood founder

O. W. Gurley was a Black landowner and entrepreneur who left Arkansas for Indian Territory and took part in land runs, including claims in the former Cherokee Outlet.

In 1906, Gurley purchased roughly forty acres of land along the Frisco tracks in north Tulsa, then a growing oil town on former Creek and Cherokee land. He platted the area, sold lots exclusively to Black buyers, and opened a rooming house on what he named Greenwood Avenue.

His investment created the core of what would become Tulsa's Greenwood District, later known as Black Wall Street.

On the ledger, Gurley represents Black migration into Indian Territory's borderlands and the deliberate use of land to carve out Black economic space in a segregated city.

J. B. Stradford

Hotel owner, legal thinker, Greenwood investor

John the Baptist Stradford was the son of a formerly enslaved man who had escaped slavery. Stradford came to Tulsa after a law degree and business experience and built one of Greenwood's landmark enterprises, the Stradford Hotel, reputed to be one of the largest Black owned hotels in the country at the time.

He also:

- bought and sold lots in Greenwood to Black settlers

- argued that Black people should build self-sufficient communities rather than depend on white institutions

- lost his hotel and much of his property in the 1921 massacre and was forced to flee under threat of prosecution

Stradford stands at the intersection of law, land, and enterprise. His life shows how legal training, property ownership, and race pride combined to build Black institutions, and how quickly white violence could strip those gains.

Buck Colbert Franklin

Lawyer, writer of the Greenwood affidavit

Buck Colbert Franklin, born in Indian Territory, practiced law in all Black towns, such as Rentiesville before moving his office to Greenwood.

After the massacre in 1921, he:

- wrote a detailed eye-witness affidavit that described airplanes dropping incendiaries and the systematic burning of the district

- joined other Black lawyers in challenging Tulsa's attempt to use new fire and zoning ordinances to prevent Black residents from rebuilding on their own land

Franklin's affidavit and legal work preserved key evidence of what happened and helped defeat a second wave of dispossession by regulation.

On the ledger, he is an example of Black professional skill used as a shield, trying to keep what little remained of a community's capital from being taken again through law rather than fire.

Modern Black Cherokee Leaders and Researchers

Guardians of the present ledger

In the present tense, Black Cherokees include tribal citizens and community advocates who are:

- serving in Cherokee Nation government and advisory roles

- working on Freedmen citizenship issues

- conducting research on Black Cherokee history, slavery, and economics

- shaping how the Nation talks about its past and allocates its resources today

Their names range from grassroots organizers to appointed officials and scholars. Together, they push the Nation to act on the 1866 treaty promise, the 2017 and 2021 court decisions, and the 2026 slavery impact study, not just in words but in budgets and programs.

They are the ones holding the pen over the current ledger.

These figures, taken together, show the arc of this book:

- from enslaved Black people whose names show up only as first names and prices,

- to the forgotten Cherokee Freedmen descendants like Ralph Treat & Charlene White whose names appear on court documents fighting to keep their citizenship

- to Black Cherokees today, who stand as citizens of the Nation and insist that the receipts from all those eras still count.

They are not side characters in Cherokee history. They are central entries in the ledger of what was built, what was taken, and what can still be repaired.

Appendix C

Glossary of Legal and Financial Terms

This glossary is here to keep the language straight. Plain words. Clear meaning. So you can see what the law was saying when it talked about people, land, and money.

Allotment

The process by which the United States broke up tribal communal land into individual parcels on paper and assigned those parcels to enrolled citizens.

In the Cherokee Nation, allotment followed the 1902 agreement. Each citizen was supposed to receive land equal in value to 110 acres of average land, with a separate homestead portion equal in value to forty acres. Allotment changed land from something held in common under tribal law to something held as individual property under federal rules.

Asset

Anything that holds value and can be owned, used, or sold.

In this book, assets include land, enslaved people as chattel in the slave era, buildings, livestock, tools, cash, and sometimes legal rights such as a lease or a contract.

Chattel slavery

A system in which human beings are treated as personal property that can be bought, sold, inherited, taxed, and used as collateral, similar to livestock or furniture.

Under chattel slavery, enslaved people had almost no recognized legal rights. Their labor and bodies were counted as assets on someone else's balance sheet.

Citizenship (Cherokee Nation)

The legal status of being a recognized member of the Cherokee Nation, with political rights such as voting and holding office, and access to certain benefits, services, and land rights.

The Treaty of 1866 required that former slaves of Cherokee citizens and certain free Blacks, and their descendants, be treated as citizens with all the rights of native Cherokees.

In the present tense, descendants of Cherokee Freedmen are Black Cherokees. They are citizens of the Cherokee Nation.

Collateral

Property pledged as a guarantee for a loan. If the borrower does not repay, the lender can take the collateral.

In this history, land, livestock, and even enslaved people under slavery could be used as collateral for debts. Later, allotment lands and Greenwood properties were also used as collateral, sometimes under unfair terms.

Communal land

Land that belongs to the Cherokee Nation as a whole rather than to individual citizens. Individuals and families can use and improve parts of it, but the underlying title belongs to the Nation.

Before allotment, most Cherokee land in both the East and Indian Territory was held this way. The Cherokee Outlet and many salt springs are examples of communal land.

Compensation

Payment given to make up for loss, damage, or harm.

Compensation can be money, land, services, or other tangible value. In this book, compensation questions arise when land is ceded, when buildings are destroyed, or when treaties promise payment for taken territory.

Deed

A written document that transfers ownership of real property, usually land and whatever is permanently attached to it.

A valid deed names the seller and buyer, describes the land, and is usually recorded at a county office. Deeds were critical in allotment and in post massacre disputes over Greenwood land.

Descendants of Cherokee Freedmen

Children, grandchildren, and later generations of the Black people who were recognized as Cherokee Freedmen under the Treaty of 1866.

In the present tense, these descendants are Black Cherokees. They are citizens of the Cherokee Nation, just as U S Freedmen descendants are Black Americans.

Emancipation

The legal ending of slavery for a specific group or in a specific jurisdiction.

The Cherokee Nation issued its own emancipation law in 1863. The Treaty of 1866 confirmed that slavery had ended and recognized Cherokee Freedmen as citizens.

Equity (wealth)

The part of an asset that you truly own, free of debt or other claims.

For example, if a house is worth 10,000 dollars and you owe 4,000 dollars on it, your equity is 6,000 dollars.

In this story, Black families often had low or fragile equity because of unfair loans, guardianship, and tax sales.

Executor and estate

An estate is the property and debts a person leaves at death. An executor is the person appointed to manage and distribute that estate under a will or court order.

In slave and allotment records, executors often sold land, livestock, and in the slave era, human beings, to pay debts. Estates were points where assets moved out of families and into the wider market.

Forfeiture

The loss of property or rights as a penalty, often without fair payment, usually because of unpaid taxes, debts, or criminal charges.

In this history, land forfeiture appears most clearly in tax sales and in certain guardianship situations.

Guardianship

A legal arrangement in which a court declares a person "incompetent" to manage their own property or affairs and appoints another person, the guardian, to manage for them.

Guardianship was used in Oklahoma to control the land and money of many Native and Black allottees, especially children and those the court labeled full blood or incompetent. In practice, some guardians sold land cheaply and kept much of the benefit.

Homestead (allotment context)

A portion of an allotment that is set aside as the family home and protected from sale or seizure for a period of time.

Under the Cherokee allotment terms, each citizen was to mark a homestead equal in value to forty acres. That portion was initially inalienable for a fixed span of years. Later federal acts changed and weakened some of these protections.

Inalienable

Property that cannot legally be sold or transferred for a set period, or sometimes permanently, without special permission.

Homestead portions of allotments were initially inalienable. Restrictions like this were supposed to protect Native land, although they also opened the door for guardianship and federal control.

Ledger

A book or digital system used to record financial transactions.

In this manuscript, the ledger is also a metaphor. It is a way of tracking value created, recorded, captured, and denied across time.

Liability

A legal responsibility or obligation to do something, usually to pay a debt or compensate for harm.

Insurance companies, governments, and individuals can all have liabilities. In the Tulsa massacre, insurers and governments largely refused to accept liability for the destruction of Greenwood.

Per capita distribution

A payment in which a communal pot of money is divided into equal shares and paid directly to each eligible person.

In the Cherokee Nation, per capita questions arose when the Cherokee Outlet was leased or sold. Fights over whether Cherokee Freedmen were included in those distributions are central to this book's theme of who gets paid.

Property (real and personal)

Real property is land and anything fixed to it, such as buildings and certain long-term improvements.

Personal property is everything else. Livestock, furniture, tools, cash, and under chattel slavery, enslaved people, were treated as personal property.

Reparations

Measures taken to repair past harms, especially large-scale injustices such as slavery, land theft, or racially motivated violence.

Reparations can include direct payments, land return, community investment, public apologies, legal changes, and other forms of material and symbolic repair.

In this narrative, reparations debates arise around both Cherokee slavery and the destruction of Greenwood.

Restricted land

Land that is subject to special rules limiting sale, lease, or taxation, usually under federal Indian law.

Restricted status was supposed to protect Native land from quick loss. Laws in the early 1900s tied the presence or absence of restrictions to blood quantum and to categories such as "Freedman," which made many Black owned allotments more vulnerable.

Riot clause (insurance)

A provision in some insurance policies that excludes coverage for damage caused by riots or civil commotion.

After the 1921 Tulsa Race Massacre, insurance companies used riot clauses to deny claims from Greenwood property owners, arguing that the destruction was the result of a riot. This allowed them to avoid paying for fire losses they would likely have covered under other circumstances.

Slavery

A system in which one person claims ownership over another, controlling their labor, movement, and family relationships through law, violence, and custom.

In this book, slavery refers to Black chattel slavery in the Cherokee Nation, where Black people were legally treated as property and could be taxed, sold, and inherited.

Treaty

A binding agreement between sovereign governments.

Here, treaty usually means agreements between the United States and the Cherokee Nation. The Treaty of 1866 is especially important because it abolished slavery in the Nation and recognized Cherokee Freedmen and their descendants as citizens.

Trust (land and money)

In Indian law, trust land is land the federal government holds legal title to for the benefit of a tribe or individual Native person.

More generally, a trust is a legal arrangement in which one party holds property for the benefit of another.

Trust ideas show up in allotment, tribal land status, and in modern proposals to manage reparation or development funds for communities like Greenwood.

Unearned advantage

A benefit or gain that a person or group receives not because of their own work, but because of their position in a system that favors them.

In this history, unearned advantages include:

- slaveholding families starting with large capital built from unpaid Black labor
- white settlers receiving Cherokee land at discounted prices

- insurance companies keeping premiums while refusing to pay out rightful claims

The term is not an insult. It is a way of naming how the ledger has been tilted.

Valuation

The process of estimating how much something is worth in money.

Valuation appears in:

- census and agency reports that put dollar values on enslaved people, houses, and livestock

- claims processes after removal and after the Tulsa massacre

- appraisals used for taxes, insurance, or sales

Who does the valuation, and under what rules, often decides whether a person or community is made whole or shortchanged.

These terms are the toolkit behind the story. They are how officials wrote our lives into law and into the books.

Knowing what the words mean is one way to make sure that, the next time those terms are used, Black Cherokees and their allies are the ones holding the pen.

Notes

Chapter 1: Slavery in the Cherokee Nation: An Economic System

1. On the early adoption of Black chattel slavery among Cherokee elites in the Southeast, see Theda Perdue, *Slavery and the Evolution of Cherokee Society, 1540–1866* (Knoxville: University of Tennessee Press, 1979).

2. Tiya Miles, *Ties That Bind: The Story of an Afro-Cherokee Family in Slavery and Freedom*, 2nd ed. (Berkeley: University of California Press, 2015), provides detailed family level examples of enslaved labor shaping Cherokee wealth.

3. For plantation scale operations at Diamond Hill and New Echota, see Tiya Miles, *The House on Diamond Hill: A Cherokee Plantation Story* (Chapel Hill: University of North Carolina Press, 2010).

4. On the valuation of enslaved people as taxable property and liquid assets in the Nation, see R. Halliburton, Jr., *Red over Black: Black Slavery among the Cherokee Indians* (Westport: Greenwood Press, 1977), and Annie Heloise Abel, *The American Indian as Slaveholder and Secessionist* (Lincoln: University of Nebraska Press, 1992).

Chapter 2: People as Property: How Wealth Was Measured

1. For slave schedules, estate inventories, and Cherokee uses of enslaved people as collateral, see R. Halliburton, Jr., *Red over Black*, and collections listed under "Cherokee Nation Papers" in the Western History Collections, University of Oklahoma.

2. On the use of enslaved labor in ferries, mills, and taverns, see Don L. Shadburn, *Cherokee Planters in Georgia, 1832–1838* (Roswell: WH Wolfe Associates, 1990).

3. On enslaved people who purchased their own freedom in Cherokee courts, including Prince and Dorcas Buffington, see Cherokee Supreme Court dockets and the Dawes testimonial materials cited in the Sequoyah Research Center holdings.

Chapter 3: Removal as Asset Destruction

1. For the economic reading of removal and the 1838 claims process, see Theda Perdue and Michael D. Green, *The Cherokee Nation and the Trail of Tears* (New York: Viking, 2007).

2. Leonard A. Carlson and Mark A. Roberts, "Indian Lands, Squatterism, and Slavery: Economic Interests and the Passage of the Indian Removal Act of 1830," *Explorations in Economic History* 43, no. 3 (2006): 486–504, provides a quantitative discussion of land value and removal politics.

Chapter 4: Forced Reconstruction in Indian Territory

1. On rebuilding in Indian Territory and the role of slave and later Freedmen labor in public buildings, see Ellen Dement Hurd, "Rebuilding a Nation: Cherokee Tribal Architecture, 1839–1907" (M.S. thesis, University of Washington, 2019).

2. For Salines, mills, and enslaved labor in Cherokee industrial sites, see Barbara Krauthamer, *Black Slaves, Indian Masters: Slavery, Emancipation, and Citizenship in the Native American South* (Chapel Hill: University of North Carolina Press, 2013).

Chapter 5: Freedom, Citizenship, and the Cost of Belonging

1. On the Treaty of 1866 and Cherokee Freedmen citizenship, see Daniel F. Littlefield Jr., *The Cherokee Freedmen: From Emancipation to American Citizenship* (Norman: University of Oklahoma Press, 1978).

2. On internal Cherokee debates over race, sovereignty, and citizenship, see Fay A. Yarbrough, *Race and the Cherokee Nation: Sovereignty in the Nineteenth Century* (Philadelphia: University of Pennsylvania Press, 2008).

Chapter 6: Education as Public Finance

1. For Cherokee public schooling and Freedmen schools as institutions, see Oklahoma Black Cherokees, Karen "Coody" Cooper and Ty Wilson (publisher details as in front matter), and primary materials from the Cherokee National Research Center.

Chapter 7: Who Gets Paid

1. On the Cherokee Outlet, lease revenue, and per capita controversies, see Fay A. Yarbrough, *Race and the Cherokee Nation*, and Claudio Saunt, *Unworthy Republic: The Dispossession of Native Americans and the Road to Indian Territory* (New York: W. W. Norton, 2020).

Chapter 8: Allotment: When Land Became Paper

1. On Cherokee allotment law and the 1902 agreement, see Theda Perdue, *Slavery and the Evolution of Cherokee Society*, and legal analyses in the Tulsa Law Review on Five Tribes titles.

2. On Dawes Rolls categories and their later use in restriction and tax policy, see Claudio Saunt, *Black, White, and Indian: Race and the Unmaking of an American Family* (New York: Oxford University Press, 2005).

Chapter 9: Labor That Built Value

1. For Black labor patterns in Indian Territory and early Oklahoma, see Patrick N. Minges, *Slavery in the Cherokee Nation: The Keetoowah Society and the Defining of a People, 1855–1867* (New York: Routledge, 2003), and the Indian Pioneer Papers.

Chapter 10: Entrepreneurs of the Cherokee Nation

1. On early Black business districts in Muskogee and other towns, see local surveys such as *The Historic Context for African American History in Muskogee, Oklahoma* (Muskogee city archives) and related municipal studies.

Chapter 11: Zachariah "Zack" Foreman Sr.

1. For economic case studies of Cherokee Freedmen and the Foreman family, see the Black Cherokee research datasets referenced in the Author's Note and works cited in Oklahoma Black Cherokees.

Chapter 12: Black Wall Street's Indian Territory Roots

1. On Greenwood's origins and the role of Black migrants and Freedmen, see the Tulsa City-County Library's Greenwood history collection and the Oklahoma Historical Society materials on Black towns.

Chapter 13: Rebuilding After Erasure

1. For the Tulsa Race Massacre, insurance denials, and rebuilding, see the *Final Report of the Oklahoma Commission to Study the Tulsa Race Riot of 1921* (2001) and subsequent analyses by Brookings and the Joint Economic Committee of Congress.

Chapters 14 and 15, Conclusion, Epilogue

1. These sections synthesize the above works, the Cherokee Nation's 2026 slavery impact report, and the author's Black Cherokee research matrix and datasets to present a unified ledger and atlas of Black Cherokee economic life.

Bibliography

Books

Abel, Annie Heloise. *The American Indian as Slaveholder and Secessionist.* Lincoln: University of Nebraska Press, 1992.

Abel, Annie Heloise. *The American Indian and the End of the Confederacy, 1863–1866.* Lincoln: University of Nebraska Press, 1993.

Abel, Annie Heloise. *The American Indian in the Civil War, 1862–1865.* Lincoln: University of Nebraska Press, 1992.

Carlson, Leonard A., and Mark A. Roberts. *Indian Lands, "Squatterism," and Slavery: Economic Interests and the Passage of the Indian Removal Act of 1830.* Various editions.

Cooper, Karen "Coody," and Ty Wilson. *Oklahoma Black Cherokees.* [Publication details as in front matter.]

Cumfer, Cynthia, ed. *Separate Peoples, One Land: The Minds of Cherokees, Blacks, and Whites on the Tennessee Frontier.* Chapel Hill: University of North Carolina Press, 2007.

Halliburton, R. Jr. *Red over Black: Black Slavery among the Cherokee Indians.* Westport: Greenwood Press, 1977.

Krauthamer, Barbara. *Black Slaves, Indian Masters: Slavery, Emancipation, and Citizenship in the Native American South.* Chapel Hill: University of North Carolina Press, 2013.

Littlefield, Daniel F. Jr. *The Cherokee Freedmen: From Emancipation to American Citizenship.* Norman: University of Oklahoma Press, 1978.

Miles, Tiya. *Ties That Bind: The Story of an Afro-Cherokee Family in Slavery and Freedom.* 2nd ed. Berkeley: University of California Press, 2015.

Miles, Tiya. *The House on Diamond Hill: A Cherokee Plantation Story.* Chapel Hill: University of North Carolina Press, 2010.

Minges, Patrick N. *Slavery in the Cherokee Nation: The Keetoowah Society and the Defining of a People, 1855–1867*. New York: Routledge, 2003.

Perdue, Theda. *Slavery and the Evolution of Cherokee Society, 1540–1866*. Knoxville: University of Tennessee Press, 1979.

Perdue, Theda, and Michael D. Green. *The Cherokee Nation and the Trail of Tears*. New York: Viking, 2007.

Saunt, Claudio. *Black, White, and Indian: Race and the Unmaking of an American Family*. New York: Oxford University Press, 2005.

Saunt, Claudio. *Unworthy Republic: The Dispossession of Native Americans and the Road to Indian Territory*. New York: W. W. Norton, 2020.

Shadburn, Don L. *Cherokee Planters in Georgia, 1832–1838: Historical Essays on Eleven Counties in the Cherokee Nation of Georgia*. Roswell: WH Wolfe Associates, 1990.

Yarbrough, Fay A. *Race and the Cherokee Nation: Sovereignty in the Nineteenth Century*. Philadelphia: University of Pennsylvania Press, 2008.

Articles and Theses

Carlson, Leonard A., and Mark A. Roberts. "Indian Lands, 'Squatterism,' and Slavery: Economic Interests and the Passage of the Indian Removal Act of 1830." *Explorations in Economic History* 43, no. 3 (2006): 486–504.

Davis, J. B. "Slavery in the Cherokee Nation." *Chronicles of Oklahoma* 11 (December 1933): 1056–72.

Hurd, Ellen Dement. "Rebuilding a Nation: Cherokee Tribal Architecture, 1839–1907." M.S. thesis, University of Washington, 2019.

Joint Economic Committee of Congress. *The Racial Wealth Gap and the Tulsa Race Massacre*. Washington, DC, various editions.

Government Documents and Legal Sources

Cherokee Nation. *The Principal Chief's Task Force to Examine the Impact of Slavery on Cherokee Nation's 19th Century Economy and Infrastructure: Final Report.* Tahlequah, OK: Cherokee Nation, January 27, 2026.

Cherokee Nation. *Constitution of the Cherokee Nation,* as amended and approved by the United States Department of the Interior, 2021.

United States. *Treaty with the Cherokee, 1866.* 14 Stat. 799.

United States. *Agreement with the Cherokee (Five Tribes Allotment Agreement).* 1902.

Oklahoma Commission to Study the Tulsa Race Riot of 1921. *Final Report.* Oklahoma City, 2001.

Archival Collections and Primary Sources

Andrew Nave Papers. John Vaughan Library, Northeastern State University, Tahlequah, OK.

Cherokee Nation Papers, WHC-M-943. Western History Collections, University of Oklahoma, Norman, OK.

Foreman Family Collection, CNC-MSS 57. Cherokee National Research Center, Tahlequah, OK.

Lulah Ross Henderson Collection of John Ross Papers and Photographs, CNC-MSS 86. Cherokee National Research Center, Tahlequah, OK.

Indian Pioneer Papers, WHC-M-309. Western History Collections, University of Oklahoma, Norman, OK.

Penelope Johnson Allen Cherokee Collection, Tennessee State Library and Archives, Nashville, TN.

Dawes Commission Enrollment and Allotment Jackets. National Archives and Records Administration.

Cherokee Phoenix and *Cherokee Advocate* newspapers, various issues.

Reports and Local Studies

Tulsa Race Riot Commission. *Final Report.* Oklahoma City, 2001.

Tulsa City-County Library. *History of Greenwood.* Tulsa, OK.

City of Muskogee. *The Historic Context for African American History in Muskogee, Oklahoma.* Muskogee, OK.

Brookings Institution. Reports on the Tulsa Race Massacre and Black wealth in Tulsa.

Appendix D

Impact of Slavery on the Cherokee Nation's 19th Century Economy and Infrastructure Final Report of the Principal Chief's Task Force
January 27, 2026

Cherokee Freedmen Monument Illustration

Courtesy of Cherokee Nation Artist Stanley Boydston

"This monument symbolizes the thousands of Cherokee Freedmen and their descendants, whose contributions, presence, and legacy have always been woven into the fabric of the Cherokee Nation. Our stories, like this image, are layered with history, culture, and the Cherokee syllabary, reminding us that we are not just a part of the past, but vital to our future within the Cherokee Nation."
— Melissa Payne

Introduction

The Cherokee Nation (the Nation), through Executive Order 2020-05 and its 2024 addendum, has reaffirmed its commitment to equal opportunity and to addressing historical patterns of disenfranchisement, including those affecting Cherokee citizens of Freedmen descent.

To begin this work, the Principal Chief convened a task force to examine how Black chattel slavery shaped the Nation's nineteenth century economy, infrastructure, and historical narrative. This report summarizes the task force's initial findings, references, and recommendations.

The full charge establishing the Principal Chief's Task Force to Examine the Impact of Slavery on Cherokee Nation's Nineteenth Century Economy and Infrastructure follows.

Task Force Charge

By Executive Order 2020-05 (Order on Equality) and the 2024 Executive Order Addendum, it is in the best interest of the Cherokee Nation to ensure that equal opportunity and equal protection under the law are at the forefront of policymaking, programs, and initiatives.

It is the policy of the Principal Chief and the Executive Branch to consider any historical acts of disenfranchisement, exclusion, or unequal treatment of groups within Cherokee society, including Cherokee citizens of Freedmen descent.

It is in Cherokee Nation's national interest to study and examine the impact of Black chattel slavery, beginning with a threshold examination of economic and infrastructure-related subjects. Understanding the Nation's use of slave labor in building the Nation, both physically in terms of building structures and in the economy and socio-economic makeup of the Cherokee Nation, ensures this is included in the greater narrative of Cherokee history.

Relatedly, Cherokee Nation must examine how slavery is depicted, interpreted, and otherwise described at its historical sites and in published materials. Therefore, the Principal Chief's Task Force to Examine the Impact of Slavery on Cherokee Nation's Nineteenth Century Economy and Infrastructure is hereby established.

Overview of Task Force Work Plan

The task force sought to examine the impact of Black chattel slavery on the nineteenth century Cherokee Nation economy and infrastructure development through a thorough review of historic auction and market records, as well as archival data related to the sale of enslaved individuals.

This required an understanding of the use of slave labor in Cherokee Nation prior to, during, and following the forced removal of Cherokees and their slaves from their eastern homelands. Additionally, the task force sought to examine the impact of slavery on the socio-economic makeup of Cherokee Nation and the tribe's intellectual ties to slavery.

The task force also reviewed how slavery is depicted, interpreted, presented, or omitted at Cherokee-owned and operated historic sites and in Cherokee Nation authored and published works or other materials.

Furthermore, a register for Cherokee Nation constructed buildings and structures built with slave labor will be created, and recommendations for areas of further study will be made.

The task force sought to research each of the areas outlined in the executive order and to produce a report identifying basic facts, providing informative yet summary answers, raising questions, and acknowledging the need for deeper inquiry. Weekly meetings were held to discuss research updates and key findings. A list of research materials identified and used by the task force is attached to the end of this report.

Executive Summary

The adoption and use of slave labor in Cherokee Nation provided a distinct economic advantage to slaveholders as compared to their non-slaveholding counterparts.

Prior to the forced removal of Cherokees from their eastern homelands, slavery was practiced in both the East in Cherokee Nation and in the Western Cherokee Nation among the Old Settlers.

The adoption of slave labor caused a socioeconomic shift in Cherokee Nation by creating class and cultural divisions that previously did not exist. This information is reflected in the 1835 census and the 1838 claims that were completed prior to removal.

Slave labor was used both pre-removal and post removal to construct homes, businesses, and government buildings.

Historical Summary

According to documented accounts, the practice of Black chattel slavery occurred in Cherokee Nation as early as the late eighteenth century.

Although slave labor was used primarily for agricultural purposes, the income earned by slaveowners was used to diversify business investments to include taverns, inns, ferries, and mills, and one can infer that slave labor was used to operate these businesses as well.

Slave labor was also used for general house duties such as cleaning, cooking, and caretaking, and in skilled trades such as brickmaking.

There is little information available on Cherokee citizens participating in slave auctions and markets. However, it is likely that Cherokees purchased individuals from the Charleston and Augusta or Hamburg markets due to their proximity.

After the federal government's ban on the importation of enslaved individuals in 1808, slaveowners in Cherokee Nation relied on natural increase, local markets, and marshals' sales as their primary sources to purchase enslaved individuals.

In addition to Cherokees purchasing and selling enslaved people, there is documentation of enslaved individuals, such as Prince (1834) and Dorcas Buffington (1856), utilizing the Cherokee legal and economic systems to purchase their own freedom.

Data shows a distinct increase in wealth among slaveholders. While some data exists on the monetary values of individual slaves (in the form of purchase prices at public sales or rewards for the return of runaway slaves), there is little information available to illustrate effectively the market rate of procuring slave labor across Cherokee Nation outside of a few individual bills of sale.

The valuation information located by the task force is listed in the table below.

Selected Valuation Records

1819

100-dollar reward – Robert, a runaway mulatto believed to be headed for the Cherokee Nation along the Arkansas River. *Source: Louisianian, June 5, 1819*

1829

Sold to highest bidder – one man named Peter, levied as property to satisfy a bond. *Source: Cherokee Phoenix, June 24, 1829*

1830

Rachel (age 9), Tom (age 7), Joe (age 6), and Clarressa (age 5) are sold from Robert B. Vann to George C. Benge for an undisclosed sum. *Source: Henderson Collection, Cherokee National Research Center*

1831

Public auction, sold to highest bidder on a credit of 12 months – two boys (names and ages not listed). *Source: Cherokee Phoenix, October 1, 1831*

1831

Forty-dollar reward – one runaway mulatto woman (name not listed). *Source: Cherokee Phoenix, October 12, 1831*

1832

Twenty-dollar reward – one woman (name not listed). *Source: Halliburton 53 (Cherokee Phoenix, February 4, 1832)*

1832

9 dollars 12 and one-half cents – receipt for services – one hired man (name not listed) for one year by Elias Boudinot from George Lowrey. *Source: Andrew Nave Collection, John Vaughan Library Special Collections, Northeastern State University*

1834

Prince (likely the father of Lucy Prince) purchased his own freedom for 150 dollars. *Source: Cherokee Supreme Court docket, 1834, University of Tennessee Libraries*

1845

Administrator's sale – between 30 and 40 young negroes and horses belonging to the estate of Joseph Vann will be sold to the highest bidder on June 17, 1845. *Source: Arkansas Intelligencer, May 13, 1845*

1847

Mary (age 26) and her three children – Nancy (age 5), Caroline (age 4), and James (age 1) – sold by the estate of Joseph Phillips to Stand Watie for the sum of 900 dollars. *Source: Cherokee Nation Papers, Western History Collection, University of Oklahoma*

1850

Peter (age 18) is sold by Susan Coodey to John Ross for the sum of 400 dollars. *Source: John Ross Papers, Helmerich Center for American Research, Gilcrease Museum*

1850

One boy named Grigg, traded from John Rollin Ridge to Mr. Eryart or Mr. Caldwell to satisfy a mortgage payment to Stand Watie in the amount of 535 dollars. *Source: Cherokee Nation Papers, Western History Collection, University of Oklahoma*

1851

One woman, name unreadable (age 28), sold by Johnson Foreman to

Maria Colston for the sum of 650 dollars.
Source: Foreman Collection, Cherokee National Research Center

1853   **or**   **1855**

George (age 40), his son Henry (age 7), and a girl named Adeline (age 8) sold by the estate of William Coody to John Ross for the sum of 750 dollars.
Source: Henderson Collection, Cherokee National Research Center

1856

Patrice (age 37) and two boys, Andrew (age 4) and Sandy (age 2), sold by Jacob and Sebrina Croft to Stand Watie for the sum of 1,300 dollars.
Source: Cherokee Nation Papers, Western History Collection, University of Oklahoma

1856

Dorcas Buffington purchased her own freedom for an unknown amount.
Source: Dawes Testimonial Packet, National Archives and Records Administration

The adoption of slave labor caused a socio-economic shift in the Cherokee Nation by creating class and cultural divisions. The slaveholding, or planter, class comprised about 6.74 percent of households in the Cherokee Nation pre-removal and was made up largely of mixed-blood families with ties to white ancestors. This information is found in the 1835 census and the 1838 claims that were completed prior to removal.

The use of slave labor correlates to an overall shift in Cherokee Nation from a subsistence-based economy to a more capitalist approach.

During the forced removal of Cherokees from their homelands in the East, enslaved people were forced to accompany their owners. Tasks during the arduous journey included clearing obstructions from roadways, hunting and cooking, serving as watchmen, and general caretaking.

Following removal, Cherokee Nation had to rebuild in Indian Territory. Slave labor played a large part in clearing land, fencing fields, rebuilding homes, farming, and saline (salt) operations, as well as general house duties.

Unfortunately, there is no census on which to rely for demographic information such as population, number of slaves per household, or crop yields. It is reasonable to conclude that at least some slave labor was used to build government buildings such as the Supreme Court building and the seminaries, as well as homes and farms.

The concept of slavery in the Cherokee Nation evolved over time, from a practice of captivity of other Indians primarily driven by concepts of kinship, to a race-based ideology introduced by European settlers. Black chattel slavery continued to be supported by tribal law until the Cherokee Nation's Emancipation Proclamation in 1863.

Emancipation was reaffirmed in the Cherokee Nation's 1866 treaty with the federal government, but it would take many generations for Cherokee Freedmen and their descendants to obtain their full treaty-protected rights as Cherokee Nation citizens.

Note on Historical Sources

The historical record used for this report is incomplete in three ways.

First, all historical research begins with incomplete evidence, which requires careful inference or acceptance of uncertainty.

Second, the history of Native peoples, including the Cherokee Nation, is fragmented due to disrupted recordkeeping, jurisdictional changes, and losses over time.

Third, the history of Black enslaved people is even more limited, with many surviving documents reducing individuals to financial entries rather than reflecting their full humanity.

However, records such as the Cherokee Supreme Court docket and Dawes Commission testimony provide rare glimpses into individual agency, documenting instances where people like Prince and Dorcas Buffington successfully negotiated the purchase of their own freedom.

These gaps shape the evidence available and the conclusions that can be drawn.

Summary of Task Force Findings by Objective

I. Impact of Black Chattel Slavery on the Nineteenth Century Cherokee Nation Economy and Infrastructure Development

a. Cherokee Nation's economy and infrastructure development did benefit directly from the implementation and use of Black chattel slavery, starting primarily in the nineteenth century.

b. Cherokee Nation's laws, at various points in history, supported the legal establishment of slavery within Cherokee Nation until the Emancipation Proclamation in 1863.

c. Black chattel slavery served as a primary engine for the Cherokee Nation's economic transition and infrastructure growth in the nineteenth century. Federal "civilization" policies sought to transform Cherokees from a subsistence-based hunting society into "herdsmen and cultivators" who embraced private property and capital accumulation.

i.   **Infrastructure and Construction** Enslaved labor was foundational to the physical development of the Nation. Enslaved men provided the skilled and manual labor required to construct stately brick manor houses, such as the Chief Vann House

(Diamond Hill), which was intended to signal Cherokee permanence and "civilization" to white Americans.

Furthermore, enslaved workers fired the bricks used for both the Vann manor and the Cherokee Council House at New Echota. See additional structures built using slave labor under Objective IX below.

ii.   **Commercial**   **Transportation**
The development of internal commerce relied on enslaved labor to build and operate ferries (such as Vann's Ferry) and toll roads. Wealthy Cherokee entrepreneurs like James Vann used their political influence to ensure that the U.S. Federal Road passed through their land, allowing them to use enslaved labor to service travelers at inns and taverns.

iii.   **Industrial**   **and**   **Resource**   **Development**
Slavery facilitated the operation of specialized industries, including gristmills, sawmills, and whiskey stills. Salt springs, which were communal property leased for profit, were operated using enslaved labor to extract salt for sale to neighboring states.

d.   **Plantation**   **Agriculture**
Slavery created a distinct wealth gap and class stratification within the Nation. By 1835, slaveholding households (a very small percentage of the Cherokee Nation population) farmed an average of 75 acres, while non slaveholders averaged only 11 acres.

This labor allowed elite Cherokees to produce surplus cotton, corn, and livestock for export to markets as far as New Orleans.

To put this disparity in contemporary terms: if the farmland were valued at an average of 5,000 to 10,000 dollars per acre, that gap would equal between 320,000 and 600,000 dollars in land value alone.

In addition to the land value gap, there is the monetary value of crop yield as well. Using corn as an illustrative crop, the slaveholders would earn approximately 50,000 dollars more per year from their crop yield than non-slaveholding Cherokees (assuming 175 bushels per acre at 4.50 dollars per bushel).

II. Historic Auctions, Market, and Records Data Related to the Sale of Enslaved Individuals

a. There is weak documentation of original captors of Caribbean imports.

b. Pre-removal records indicate that Cherokees purchased enslaved individuals from markets in Charleston and Augusta, or Hamburg.

c. After the 1808 ban on the import of enslaved individuals, Cherokees relied on natural increase, local markets, or marshals' sales.

d. Post removal records indicate that Cherokees relied on markets along the Arkansas River corridor – primarily Van Buren (Arkansas), Fort Smith (Arkansas), and Webbers Falls (Oklahoma).

e. There is documentation of slaveholders hiring out (renting) slave labor to non-slaveholders. This created yet another stream of income for slaveholders, which served to widen the wealth gap between slaveholders and non-slaveholders.

f. Historical records from the nineteenth century establish that the Cherokee Nation treated enslaved individuals as taxable chattel property and liquid assets. These "assets" were often used to settle debts and satisfy court judgments.

i. Market Valuations

In 1809, the Cherokee Agency conducted a statistical survey valuing the Nation's 583 enslaved individuals at 300 dollars each. This 300-dollar valuation represents a significant capital investment compared to the 10 to 60 dollar valuation of a typical Cherokee log home.

By 1835, the census recorded a total of 1,592 enslaved people within the Nation, with approximately one slave for every 10.5 Cherokee citizens.

ii. Specific Auction and Record Examples

1. **The Vann Estate**
   James Vann owned 115 enslaved people in 1809, representing
   nearly 20 percent of the total enslaved population in the
   Nation at that time.

2. **Public Auctions at New Echota**
   In June 1829, Cherokee Marshal Joseph Lynch advertised the
   public sale of a "likely negro boy named George" to satisfy
   the debts of Ambrose Harnage.

3. **Bond Satisfaction Sales**
   In September 1831, Marshal Lynch auctioned "one Negro
   man named Peter" to satisfy a bond for Edward Hicks.

4. **James Pettit Judgment**
   A court-ordered sale included an enslaved man named
   Gabriel to satisfy a 500-dollar judgment against James Pettit.

5. **Estate Liquidations**
   The estate of T. B. Adair was liquidated through a twelve-
   month credit auction of "three negroes, Joe, his wife Nelly,
   and child."

6. **Inter-Tribal and External Trade**
   Cherokee planters purchased slaves from New Orleans
   markets and from white traders in Arkansas and Tennessee.
   For example, in 1838, Lewis Ross (brother of Chief John
   Ross) transported 500 slaves from Georgia to the Cherokee
   Nation for sale to other Cherokee citizens.

g. Understanding the use of slave labor in the Cherokee Nation
pre-removal.

h. Although slave labor was used primarily for agricultural
purposes, the diversification of business investments to include

taverns, inns, ferries, mills, and similar enterprises meant slave labor was used to operate these businesses.

i. It should be noted that the profits generated through slave labor, primarily agricultural labor, were used to invest in these diverse business ventures.

j. Other uses of slave labor included domestic tasks (cooking, cleaning, nursing, childcare, and related work), skilled labor (such as brickmaking), and other tasks such as translating.

III. Impact of Slavery on the Socio-Economic Makeup of Cherokee Nation

a. The institutionalization of Black chattel slavery in nineteenth century Cherokee Nation fundamentally transformed its socio-economic makeup, shifting the society from an egalitarian, subsistence-based culture to a stratified class hierarchy driven by plantation agriculture and mercantile capitalism.

b. Cherokee Nation's transition to a capitalist economy and use of slave labor created an elite planter class, small in numbers but extremely influential in the Nation's government.

c. Slavery facilitated a drastic shift in traditional gender roles. As men took on the role of plantation masters, they entered the agricultural sphere, historically a female domain, while Cherokee women were relegated to a diminished domestic sphere focused on spinning and weaving.

This shift in the domestic space coincided with the political disenfranchisement of women and the consolidation of power in a centralized republic governed by the small percentage of slaveholding men. The political influence of this class was substantial. For instance, 11 of the 12 signers of the 1827 Cherokee Constitution were slaveholders.

d. The socio-economic impact of slavery on Cherokee Nation was like the weaving of a double walled basket. The outer layer displayed the "civilized" progress of a sovereign republic. The inner structural integrity was comprised of an exploited labor force that was systematically excluded from the benefits of that very progress.

IV. Use of Slave Labor During the Forced Removal of the Cherokee People

a. The use of slave labor during the forced removal primarily benefited slaveholders, but some benefit was experienced by the larger group.

Enslaved persons cleared obstructions from roadways, cooked meals, hunted, served as night watchmen, and provided general caretaking to their owners.

V. Use of Slave Labor in Cherokee Nation Post Removal

a. The use of slave labor in Indian Territory post-removal was pivotal to the building of a new Cherokee Nation.

Enslaved people cleared land for improvements, fenced fields, cut logs for construction, built structures, constructed docks, and planted crops. Cherokee families in possession of enslaved people were able to rebuild their lives at a much faster pace than those without access to slave labor.

VI. Cherokee Nation's Intellectual Ties to Slavery

a. Cherokee Nation's intellectual ideas of slavery evolved significantly over time, from the practice of captivity of other Indians primarily driven by an absence of kinship among Cherokee communities, to an adopted system driven by capitalistic values and racial ideology from European settlers.

b. African and Cherokee cultural exchange over time occurred in areas including, but not limited to, agriculture, textile production, and regional herbal medicine.

VII. Depiction and Interpretation of Slavery at Cherokee Owned and Operated Historic Sites and in Cherokee Nation Authored and Published Works

a. The depictions and interpretation of slavery within Cherokee Nation's historic sites and museums are currently limited, largely due to the specific scope and interpretive strategy established for each site.

Of Cherokee Nation's seven museum properties, the Cherokee National History Museum is the only site that directly includes content related to slavery and Cherokee Freedmen within its interpretive materials.

b. Among the seven museums, one historic building, the Cherokee National Supreme Court Museum, was constructed prior to emancipation and has been concluded to have been built, at least in part, using slave labor under the supervision of a general contractor.

Further study is needed to determine the extent to which enslaved labor was used. However, the confirmed involvement of enslaved workers should be memorialized and incorporated into the building's interpretive narrative. At present, the museum's interpretation does not include specific content addressing slavery or Cherokee Freedmen.

c. To ensure a more complete and accurate representation of Cherokee Nation's history, it is recommended that Cherokee Nation pursue additional research on the role and experiences of enslaved people and Cherokee Freedmen across all historic sites.

Findings from this research should be integrated into a unified interpretive strategy, ensuring that the history of slavery – its impact, legacy, and connection to each site – is consistently and thoughtfully presented throughout all Cherokee Nation museums.

VIII. Creation of a Register for Cherokee Nation Constructed Buildings and Structures Built Using Slave Labor

a. Based on societal conditions of the time, it is reasonable to conclude that the following buildings were constructed, at least partially, with slave labor:

i. The Cherokee National Supreme Court Museum in Tahlequah, Oklahoma, which once housed both Cherokee Nation's judicial branch and the Cherokee Advocate offices.

- Cherokee National Historic Register (CNHR) 005

- National Register of Historic Places (NRHP) 74001657

ii. The Lewis Ross home, later the Cherokee Orphan Asylum, in Salina, Oklahoma.

- CNHR 015

- NRHP 83002092

- The springhouse is the only remaining structure.

iii. The original Cherokee Female Seminary in Park Hill, Oklahoma.

- CNHR 006

- NRHP 74001658

- Three columns of the original structure remain standing.

b. It is reasonable to include that enslaved people constructed, at least partially, private or domestic structures located within Cherokee Nation:

i. Rose Cottage in Park Hill, Oklahoma.

- CNHR 009

ii. Hunter's Home Historic Site in Park Hill, Oklahoma.

- CNHR 008

- NRHP 70000530

IX. Recommendations for Further Study

a. Recommendations for further study include, but are not limited to:

i. Research the earliest documented use of Black chattel slavery in Cherokee Nation. This will likely require investment in visits to archives in the southeastern United States.

ii. Examine Cherokee Supreme Court dockets, Dawes Commission testimonies, and pension applications to identify and document instances of self-purchase and manumission.

iii. Create a fellowship, or other such position, for a scholar or post-doctoral student to examine surviving records over a multiyear period. This will require investment in compensation for the fellow, as well as refinement of research parameters and goals.

X. Threshold Examinations and Summary

The task force was charged to conduct the foregoing examination and threshold reviews, identifying basic facts, providing informative yet summary answers, raising questions, and acknowledging the need for deeper inquiry.

This report fulfills that initial charge and points clearly to areas where sustained research and policy attention are needed.

Task Force Recommendations

1. Support In Depth Research

a. Develop a comprehensive source guide or annotated bibliography identifying archival collections, published works, and other materials related to Cherokees and slavery that require detailed review and analysis in future phases of work.

b. Support primary source research in identified repositories through employment opportunities and or a fellowship program.

c. Provide grant funding to external institutions to digitize relevant records, once identified, and ensure they are accessible for future research.

2. Establish the Register of Slave Built Structures and Develop Interpretation Protocols

Complete the planned creation of the register for Cherokee Nation constructed buildings and structures built using slave labor.

Following the establishment of this register, a focused effort should be made to examine and revise how slavery is depicted, interpreted, presented, or omitted at these identified Cherokee owned and operated historic sites.

3. Integrate Slavery and Freedmen History Across All Historic Sites

To ensure a more complete and accurate representation of Cherokee Nation's history, it is recommended that Cherokee Nation pursue additional research on the role and experiences of enslaved people and Cherokee Freedmen across all historic sites.

Findings from this research should be integrated into a unified interpretive strategy, ensuring that the history of slavery, its impact, legacy, and connection to each site is consistently and thoughtfully presented throughout all Cherokee Nation museums.

Submitted by Task Force Members

- Melissa Payne, Cherokee Freedmen Community Liaison

- Ashawna Miles, Cherokee Nation Director of Self Governance

- Shella Bowlin, Cherokee Nation Secretary of State

- Mark Harrison, Cherokee Freedmen Art and History Project Committee Member

- Tralynna Scott, Cherokee Nation Special Envoy to U.S. Department of the Treasury and Cherokee Nation Businesses Chief Economist

- Travis Owens, Cherokee Nation Businesses, Vice President of Cultural Tourism

Additional persons related to the drafting of this report:

- Adrienne McMurray, CNB Senior Administrative Assistant

- Ross Mulcare, CNB Senior Manager, Cherokee National Research Center

- Krystan Moser, CNB Senior Cultural Resource Manager

Research Materials

This is not a comprehensive list of relevant sources. The task force recommends that the development of such a list be a focus of future work.

Primary Sources

Newspapers

- *Cherokee Phoenix*

- *Cherokee Advocate*

Government Documents

- 1835 Census of Cherokees Living East of the Mississippi River ("Henderson Roll")

- 1838 Claims

Archival Collections and Documents

- Andrew Nave Papers. University Archives and Special Collections, John Vaughan Library, Northeastern State University.

- Cherokee Collection. University of Tennessee Libraries.

  Digital collection at the University of Tennessee Libraries.

- Cherokee Nation Papers Collection, WHC-M-943. Western History Collections, University of Oklahoma.

- Foreman Family Collection, CNC-MSS 57. Cherokee National Collection, Cherokee National Research Center.

  Includes "Sale of two slaves," undated (Box 1, Folder 11, Object 4b).

- Gilder Lehrman Collection, The Gilder Lehrman Institute of American History.

  Includes "Bill of sale for 47 black slaves to Michael Deloach" (GLC07369).

- Indian Pioneer Papers Collection, WHC-M-309. Western History Collections, University of Oklahoma.

- Lulah Ross Henderson Collection of John Ross Papers and Photographs, CNC-MSS 86. Cherokee National Collection, Cherokee National Research Center.

  Includes:

    - Copy of bill of sale from Robert Vann to George Benge, 12 September 1830

- Bill of sale from D. R. Coody to John Ross, 29 January 1851

    - "Act to prevent amalgamation with colored persons," 19 September 1839

- Penelope Johnson Allen Cherokee Collection, 1775–1878, Acc. 1787. Tennessee State Library and Archives.

    Includes:

    - Report of George Butler, Cherokee Agent, 1859

    - Cherokee Supreme Court docket, 1829

Secondary Sources

Books

Abel, Annie Heloise. *The American Indian and the End of the Confederacy, 1863–1866*. University of Nebraska Press, 1993.

Abel, Annie Heloise. *The American Indian as Slaveholder and Secessionist*. University of Nebraska Press, 1992.

Abel, Annie Heloise. *The American Indian in the Civil War, 1862–1865*. University of Nebraska Press, 1992.

Cumfer, Cynthia, ed. *Separate Peoples, One Land: The Minds of Cherokees, Blacks, and Whites on the Tennessee Frontier*. University of North Carolina Press, 2007.

Halliburton, R. Jr. *Red over Black: Black Slavery among the Cherokee Indians*. Greenwood Press, 1977.

Krauthamer, Barbara. *Black Slaves, Indian Masters: Slavery, Emancipation, and Citizenship in the Native American South*. University of North Carolina Press, 2013.

Miles, Tiya, ed. "African American History at the Chief Vann House." University of Michigan, 2006.

Miles, Tiya. *The House on Diamond Hill: A Cherokee Plantation Story.* University of North Carolina Press, 2010.

Miles, Tiya. *Ties That Bind: The Story of an Afro-Cherokee Family in Slavery and Freedom.* 2nd ed. University of California Press, 2015.

Minges, Patrick N. *Slavery in the Cherokee Nation: The Keetoowah Society and the Defining of a People, 1855–1867.* Routledge, 2003.

Perdue, Theda. *Slavery and the Evolution of Cherokee Society, 1540–1866.* University of Tennessee Press, 1979.

Perdue, Theda, and Michael D. Green. *The Cherokee Nation and the Trail of Tears.* Viking, 2007.

Shadburn, Don L. *Cherokee Planters in Georgia, 1832–1838: Historical Essays on Eleven Counties in the Cherokee Nation of Georgia.* WH Wolfe Associates, 1990.

Yarbrough, Fay A. *Race and the Cherokee Nation: Sovereignty in the Nineteenth Century.* University of Pennsylvania Press, 2008.

Journal Articles

Carlson, Leonard A., and Mark A. Roberts. "Indian Lands, 'Squatterism,' and Slavery: Economic Interests and the Passage of the Indian Removal Act of 1830." *Explorations in Economic History* 43, no. 3 (2006): 486–504.

Davis, J. B. "Slavery in the Cherokee Nation." *Chronicles of Oklahoma* 11 (December 1933): 1056–72.

Theses and Dissertations

Hurd, Ellen Dement. "Rebuilding a Nation: Cherokee Tribal Architecture, 1839–1907." M.S. Thesis, University of Washington, 2019.

Series Mission Statement

The Black Cherokee Series exists to restore the full, unbroken story of Black Cherokees. including free Black families who lived in Cherokee society before removal, Black people who married into Cherokee families and raised Cherokee descendants, and the Cherokee Freedmen and their descendants whose citizenship was guaranteed under the Treaty of 1866.

This series challenges colonial narratives, exposes the harm of roll based identity, and centers the lived experiences of the people whose names were too often reduced to "et al." It honors the elders, ancestors, and descendants who carried Cherokee identity through silence, suspicion, and struggle.

The mission is simple:

To tell the truth.

To restore the record.

To honor the people.

To ensure Black Cherokee history is recognized as Cherokee history.

Find more Cherokee books by CBIHP members at

www.cbihpfoundation.org/cbihp-books.html

You can also scan the QR code above.

About the Author

Ty "GWY" Wilson is a citizen of the Cherokee Nation, a Cherokee historian, author, filmmaker, artist, and community advocate from Tahlequah, Oklahoma. Raised in the Lee Street neighborhood, the last predominantly Black Cherokee neighborhood of Tahlequah in the late 1900's, he grew up inside Cherokee life and carries that world into everything he creates.

He is the founder and president of the Cherokees for Black Indian History Preservation Foundation, serves on the Cherokee Nation Freedmen History Advisory Committee, and sits on the board of the Oklahoma Blues Hall of Fame. Ty is editor and contributing writer of *Oklahoma Black Cherokees* and author of *1st American: Cherokee, 1st American: Keetoowah,* and *1st American: Choctaw* which are part of a Children's book series to preserve Native American languages. He is also the author of *Cherokee Freedmen: We Are Cherokee and the Ledger and The Land; Slavery, Wealth, and the Black Cherokee Economy Before and After Removal,* which are part of his "BLACK CHEROKEE" series.

Across his work as an author, jewelry maker, photographer, songwriter, filmmaker, poet, and community advocate, Ty's purpose is steady: to honor the elders, families, and neighbors of his Oklahoma communities, and to ensure that Native American stories are preserved in their full truth.